THE ECONOMIC ORGANISATION
OF ENGLAND

BY THE SAME AUTHOR.

AN INTRODUCTION TO ENGLISH ECONOMIC
HISTORY AND THEORY. Crown 8vo.
Part I. THE MIDDLE AGES. 7s. 6d. net.
Part II. THE END OF THE MIDDLE AGES. 14s. net.

THE ADJUSTMENT OF WAGES: a Study in the
Coal and Iron Industries of Great Britain and America.
With 4 Maps. 8vo. 14s. net.

BRITISH DOMINIONS: THEIR PRESENT
COMMERCIAL AND INDUSTRIAL CONDITION. A
Series of General Reviews for Business Men and Students.
Edited by SIR WILLIAM ASHLEY. Crown 8vo. 7s. 6d. net.

POLITICAL ECONOMY. By JOHN STUART MILL.
With an introduction by SIR WILLIAM ASHLEY. Crown 8vo.
7s. 6d. net.

The Economic Organisation of England

An Outline History

By

Sir William Ashley

PH.D., M.A., M.COM.

Professor of Commerce in the University of Birmingham;
Late Professor of Economic History in Harvard University;
Sometime Fellow of Lincoln College, Oxford

WILDSIDE PRESS

PREFACE

THE following lectures are printed substantially as they were delivered in the fortnight before Christmas 1912, as part of the "general lecture system" attached to the Colonial Institute of Hamburg. They are on the lines of a brief course which I have been in the habit of giving for the last few years at the University of Birmingham.

For the purpose which I have had in view, I hope the brevity of this book will be regarded as a merit. I venture to think it may be of some advantage to those who approach for the first time the subject of English economic history, to be furnished with a narrative which gives them a general notion of a great part of the ground to be covered and of many of the topics they will have to consider.

EDGBASTON, *April* 1914.

CONTENTS

LECTURE	PAGE
I. The English Agrarian System: the Manor as Starting Point	1
II. The Stages of Industrial Evolution: the Gild as Starting Point	25
III. The Beginnings of Modern Farming: the Break-up of the Manor	44
IV. The Rise of Foreign Trade: the Advent of Capital and Investment	68
V. Domestic Industry and Tudor Nationalism	88
VI. Agricultural Estates and English Self-Government	119
VII. The Industrial Revolution and Freedom of Contract	140
VIII. Joint Stock and the Evolution of Capitalism	173
Appendix—Suggestions for Further Reading	193
Index	207

The Economic Organisation of England

LECTURE I

The English Agrarian System: the Manor as Starting Point

IN this course of lectures I propose to direct your attention mainly, though not exclusively, to the forms of economic organisation, as illustrated by English development. Economic history, the history of man's economic activity, is the history of the utilisation by man of his environment, to obtain therefrom subsistence and the satisfaction of those material wants which are bound up with subsistence. But his activity in this direction, from the very dawn of history, has never been entirely individualistic; never altogether the operation of absolutely isolated individuals. Some form of association has always been in existence, it would appear, since man became man; and this has involved some sort, however rudimentary, of distribution of functions—some form, in short, of organisation. Economic history is an exceedingly wide and complex subject, even for one nation for a few centuries of its career. We cannot hope to deal

Economic Organisation

satisfactorily with it in a short course : much indeed of it is still so imperfectly known to us that we could hardly hope to deal with it quite satisfactorily, in the present state of our knowledge, however many lectures were assigned to it. But by taking for our special theme the forms of organisation and their changes, we may find threads which will guide us, at any rate through that part of the labyrinth which I am going to ask you to tread.

I shall begin with agricultural conditions ; and this for two reasons. The first is that, like all the rest of western Europe, England, until a couple of centuries ago, was an almost exclusively agricultural country. One of our tasks will be to show the way in which England, from being an agricultural country, supplying itself with food, has become primarily a manufacturing country, dependent upon importation for its sustenance. The other reason is that hitherto the agrarian development of England has been unique in western Europe. All over western and central Europe, in the twelfth and thirteenth centuries, the land was cultivated by serfs bound to the soil. Outside England, the descendants or representatives of these serfs still remain on the land, in all but a few districts ; either as "peasant proprietors," owning the acres they till, or as small tenant farmers with something closely approaching in practice to permanence of tenure. In Germany, as a whole, between two-thirds and three-quarters of the land is still owned and cultivated by peasants : peasant properties occupy from two-fifths to two-thirds of the area even of those provinces east of the Elbe which most nearly resemble England in the predominance of large

English Agrarian System

owners; while in the south-west of the empire peasant properties monopolise almost the whole country. In France large estates are distributed more evenly over the several provinces; but in that country, also, quite one-half of the whole land is still in the hands of peasant owners. In England, on the contrary, by far the larger part of the cultivable area has come to be owned by comparatively few "landlords." There are still, it is true, a very large number of separate owners: counting urban and rural together, there are said to be as many as a million in England and Wales. But very many of their properties are quite small, and make up, in the aggregate, but an inconsiderable proportion of the total area. Before the recent "agricultural depression," from which the country is now emerging, it was calculated—and no substantial change in the situation has, as yet, taken place—that 4,200 persons owned between them considerably more than half the soil of England and Wales, and that the owners of the other half, so far as it was really agricultural land, numbered no more than 34,000.

We realise even more distinctly the uniqueness of modern English conditions when we learn that the peculiarity of England extends beyond the actual ownership of the soil. It consists in "the three-fold division of agricultural interests,"—the fact, that is, that three classes are usually associated with the cultivation of the land, and expect to derive an income from it —landlords, tenant farmers, and agricultural labourers. The landlord is hardly ever a merely passive receiver of rent: he provides farm houses, barns and sheds, fencing, and usually a good deal of drainage. He charges himself

Economic Organisation

not only with upkeep, but also, from time to time, with extensive improvements ; and though there are doubtless impoverished landlords here and there who do very little, the average expenditure for these purposes on what is called a well-managed estate commonly amounts to a quarter or even more of the gross rent. The owner lets the bulk of his land in comparatively large holdings—150 or 200 acres being perhaps the more usual size in the centre of the country—receiving a rent determined in the main by competition. The tenant farmer provides his own stock and implements and working capital, and, compared with most of the peasant cultivators abroad, is something of a "capitalist;" and he employs agricultural labourers, who may indeed rent cottages on easy terms, and have the use of gardens or allotments, but nevertheless depend chiefly on their wages. Each of these classes may be paralleled from one or other province of France, Germany, or Italy. In some districts there are great landlords ; but then they usually, as in eastern Germany, cultivate the greater part of their estates themselves, personally or through bailiffs ; or, as commonly in Italy and in certain departments of France, they let them out in small holdings to peasant cultivators, who employ little labour outside their own families. These peasant tenants are very frequently what are known as *métayers*, paying, in lieu of a money rent, some fraction, ordinarily one-half, of the annual produce. There are districts again, as in the north of France, where tenants may be found, superficially not unlike English farmers in their position : but they usually have a smaller command of capital ; they obtain less

English Agrarian System

trom their landlords in the way of repairs and capital expenditure; and their landlords are frequently townsmen, who are altogether urban in their outlook and chief interests. And, finally, in most districts abroad there are agricultural labourers; but most of them are engaged by employers who are themselves, whether on a large or a small scale, the proprietors of the land on which they work. Hardly anywhere on the Continent can one find on the same land all three classes, each participating, as in England, in the task of production. And to discover when, and, if it may be, why, England diverged in this important respect from the rest of Europe furnishes one of the main interests of English economic history, and a reason for beginning with the agricultural side of it.

The characteristic figure for the last couple of centuries, if not longer, has been "the squire" of the village. There are signs, as an eminent English statesman has recently remarked, that the squire is now beginning to pass away. But certainly he has for a long time been firmly rooted in English soil. And for what the squire has meant let us turn to the following description by Lord Eversley of "the ideal of the English land system"—the ideal, that is to say, in the eyes of the land-owning gentry.

Writing some twenty years ago—and since then things have altered but little—he tells us:—"The ideal of the English land system . . . is that of a large estate where the whole of one and often of several adjoining parishes is included in it; where there is no other landowner within the ring fence; where the village itself belongs to the same owner as the agri-

Economic Organisation

cultural land; where all the people of the district—farmers, tradesmen, labourers—are dependent, directly or indirectly, on the one landowner, the farmers holding their land from him, generally on a yearly tenancy, the labourers hiring their cottages weekly or yearly either from the landowner or from the farmers; and where the village tradespeople are also dependent largely for their custom on the squire of the district, and hold their houses from him. It is believed that this ideal has practically been attained in more than half the rural parishes of England and Wales, in the sense that all the land and houses within them substantially belong in each to a single owner. In a very large number of cases a single landowner possesses the whole of several adjoining parishes or of several parishes in different parts of the country."

It is not my present business to endeavour to sum up the relative merits and demerits of such an agrarian system from the social point of view. It is sufficient to say that, before it encountered the competition of the virgin soil of the new world, it was associated with methods of agriculture which competent foreign observers held up as models to be imitated by their own countries. There can be no doubt whatever that it did actually promote production. "English agriculture, taken as a whole," wrote the highest French authority in 1854, "is, at this day, the first in the world; and it is in the way of realising further progress." In spite of an inferior soil and climate, the gross produce, he reckoned, per acre was at least twice as great in England as in France. The chief German authority has been equally emphatic. "England, the

English Agrarian System

country most evidently characterised by large landed estates, was," he tells us, "justly regarded from the end of the eighteenth to the middle of the nineteenth century, as the High School of agriculture." Moreover, though it is hardly possible to deny the advantages which a country derives from the presence of a peasant proprietary, it is easy to paint the material position of such a class in modern Europe in colours somewhat too rosy. The drawbacks may be easily discerned in what is still the best general account of their position, the two eulogistic chapters in the *Political Economy* of John Stuart Mill. What we have now to do, however, is simply to trace the origin and development of the modern English system. The basis on which it was built was feudal: it grew out of the manorial system, which was a fundamental part of European feudalism in the period when feudalism reached its highest development. In a sense it is a survival of feudalism; and England, though it plumes itself on the absence of a noble caste, may be not inaptly described as more feudal to-day than France or Germany. But France and Germany also had their manorial system in the Middle Ages. The remarkable fact is that squiredom in England, though it rested on the feudal basis of the manor, was built up to its modern completeness very largely as the result of forces which we commonly regard as non-feudal, viz. Commerce and the Reformation and Parliamentary Government. How this happened we shall have to see later. We must now look at the foundation, the manorial system itself.

For this purpose I shall not go further back than

Economic Organisation

the thirteenth century. It is quite certain that by that time, whatever may have been the case before, the whole of agricultural England was divided into areas known as "manors," though these were of very unequal size: and over the larger part of England, especially the Midlands and the South, there was a remarkable similarity in their constitution, so that, in reference to these districts at any rate, we are justified in speaking of a "typical" or "normal" manor. The typical manor consisted of a village, with the lands surrounding it which the villagers cultivated. Every manor had a lord, either a lay lord or an ecclesiastical corporation, though sometimes a manor was divided between two or more lords. And the manor was the unit of land management. A magnate might possess scores of manors in various parts of the country; two of the kinsmen of William the Conqueror, for instance, were given more than four hundred manors, and one almost double that number. But all such great estates were thought of as still made up of a number of separate manors, each with its own internal arrangements and its own separate system of associated husbandry. There were, it is true, certain large complexes of property, known as "baronies" and "honours." These would be under the supervision of "seneschals" or "stewards," who made periodical circuits to see that the local estate officials were doing their duty. In some cases the several manors sent each year prescribed quantities of provisions to the monastery or to the "head manor" where their lord, whether corporate or individual, resided. But all this left untouched the internal working of each several manor,

The Manor

which continued complete and self-contained within itself.

The position of affairs, so far as landlordship was concerned, seems at once intelligible to the modern Englishman, because the mediæval lord of the manor is evidently represented by the modern squire of the village. Many great landlords of to-day own, each of them, all the land of several parishes, which are often widely separated: while in many villages the position of squire is occupied by the Ecclesiastical Commissioners, by the colleges of Oxford and Cambridge, and by the great hospitals, just as that of lord of the manor was held in the thirteenth century by cathedral or monastic foundations. But there are two great differences between the mediæval and the modern state of affairs—one external, and relating to the theory of landholding; the other internal, and relating to the methods of husbandry.

To take the external first. To-day we apply the term "tenants" only to those who have hired land of a landlord; and whatever may still be the theory of English law, we do, in fact, regard landlords as absolute owners of their land and as tenants of no man. But in the Middle Ages the lords of manors themselves were "tenants." As the Latin original of "tenants" implies, they were "holders" of land from a superior. All land was held ultimately of the king, except of course the king's own estates; but the connection was not necessarily an immediate one. It has been calculated that, at the time of the Domesday Survey (1086), there were about eight thousand lords

Economic Organisation

of land who were sub-tenants, holding of some lord intermediate between themselves and the king; while there were only about fourteen hundred persons holding directly of the king—or, as they were called, "tenants in chief"; many of them, no doubt, great lords, lay or ecclesiastical, but many, also, holders of but one or two manors. Somewhere about one-fifth of the land of the country was then retained in the hands of the crown; rather more, perhaps three-tenths, was held by ecclesiastics and ecclesiastical bodies; and the other half was divided between lay lords. Little change in these proportions would seem to have taken place during the Middle Ages. And all the lay holders of manors, at any rate—not to complicate the subject by considering the ecclesiastical owners—held their manors on condition of performing certain services to their lord, whether the king or some intermediate superior, and of submitting to certain conditions incidental to their tenure. The service due was mainly military service; so that they were said to be "tenants in chivalry"; and the chief other "incidents" of this tenure were submission to the lord's rights of wardship over an heir while under age, and of providing for an heiress in marriage—rights which were originally of considerable pecuniary value. The theory of "tenure" was a fundamental part of mediæval feudalism; but it has since ceased to have any real meaning. Military service, as a condition of landlordship, passed away completely in the seventeenth century, when a paid army came into existence; it had long been a mere shadow of its former self. And the other incidents of tenure in chivalry

The Manor

were abolished by the parliaments of the Commonwealth and Charles the Second, and the loss to the royal revenue compensated for by "the hereditary excise."

The lord of the manor, in the course of his transformation into the squire of the village, has thus been freed from his dependence upon a superior lord. We have now to follow what has happened within the manor itself; and for that purpose some further description is necessary of its internal constitution in the thirteenth century.

The usual manor of the Midlands and South of England consisted of a village, or "town," with several hundreds of acres of arable land surrounding it. In this village lived all the cultivators of the soil: the isolated farm-house we are now accustomed to is a comparatively late innovation. Beyond the arable fields lay considerable stretches of pasture and waste, and of woodland where the swine foraged for food: if there were a stream near by, there would also be a tract of permanent meadow. It was an organisation primarily for tillage—for arable husbandry; pastoral occupations were for a long time altogether secondary and subsidiary; and the use of meadow and pasture and waste was regarded as "appurtenant" to the use of the arable fields. There have been certain geographers in recent years who have thought that, over a large part of the area of England, tillage was physically a mistake; and that the laying down of cornfields to pasture, which took place so widely in Tudor times and again in recent years, was but a belated concession to a damp climate. Whether this be so or no, the manorial system, in the complete form which is here

Economic Organisation

being described, was never thoroughly at home in the western side of England, where pasture farming was dictated by soil and rainfall. This, and not any Celtic origin of its inhabitants, is probably the reason for the absence, over a large part of the western counties, of the compact and substantial village with its wide arable fields—the so-called "nucleated" village—and the presence, in its place, of tiny hamlets and scattered homesteads.

To return, however, to the normal manor. It had three remarkable characteristics. One was the division of the whole arable area into two portions—that part (perhaps a third or half of the whole) which was kept in the hands of the lord and cultivated under his direction, or that of a bailiff or reeve representing him, for his direct and exclusive benefit; and the rest of the land, which was in the hands of tenants. The former part was universally known as the "demesne"; the latter was known by various names, of which "land in villeinage" was the most common. The term "demesne" survives in a somewhat similar sense in Ireland; and we have no difficulty in thinking of it as similar to the modern "home farm," which a landlord keeps in his own possession and manages himself or through a bailiff; though the demesne constituted as a rule a far larger portion of the manor than the home farm does of a modern "estate."

But now we come to a second and more significant characteristic: the fact that the labour necessary for the demesne was provided by the tenants of the rest of the manor. Besides extra services, commonly known as "boondays," at harvest time and other seasons of

The Manor

exceptional pressure, and also a good deal of compulsory carting, the main body of the tenants—those known as "villagers" *par excellence* (for that is what "villeins" seems originally to have meant)—were bound to work (or provide a substitute) on two or three days a week all the year round on the lord's demesne. This was the so-called "week work"; and it will be at once realised what an immensely important factor such an obligation must have been in the whole of rural life. The services can, if we like, be described as the "rent" paid to the lord for the use of the land; or the use of the land can be described as the "wages" paid by the lord for the villein's services: in truth, neither "rent" nor "wages" are appropriate to the circumstances, since, among other reasons, the arrangement rested much more on custom and status than on competition and contract. It should be added, for completeness' sake, that the tenants were often bound to make certain small periodical payments in kind, such as poultry or eggs: but, by the side of the labour dues, obligations such as these were quite inconsiderable.

The third characteristic is even more remote from anything with which we are now familiar. It was that the holdings of the villeins were made up, not of compact "fields," each several acres in extent, such as we are now accustomed to, but of a number of acre or half-acre strips, scattered over the whole of the tilled area. This tilled area was divided into two, three, or four—most commonly three—great expanses, known in later times as "open" fields, because over the whole of each there was no hedge or ditch or wall

Economic Organisation

or fence to obstruct the view, and the strips were only separated by low "balks" of unploughed turf. The division into two, three, or four "fields" was for the purpose of a systematic fallowing,—one half, third, or fourth, as the case might be, being left untilled each year,—and to permit of a rude rotation of crops. On the three-field plan, which was by far the most usual in the thirteenth and subsequent centuries in England, one of the fields would be sown in the autumn with rye or wheat (the bread crop), one in the spring with barley (the drink crop), or with oats or beans or peas for the cattle; while the third was left fallow. The rotation in each manor was absolutely compulsory on all sharers in the open field. In Germany, where the open field is still widely prevalent, there is a convenient technical term, *Feldzwang*, "field compulsion." In mediæval England there was no similar term, doubtless because the rule was so much a matter of course that it did not need to be named.

And in each manor there was, at this time, a usual or characteristic size of villein's holding, known by various significant names, such as "husbandland," "living," and the like, but most commonly, from the measuring rod or yard (*virga*), as a "yardland" or, in Latin, as a "virgate." Its size varied from place to place very considerably; but certainly by far the most usual size was thirty (scattered) acres: in a three-field village the "full villein" would have approximately ten acres in each field, no two being contiguous. The "acre" was seldom of precisely the extent of the modern statute acre, but varied according to local custom, the nature of the soil, and the lie of the land.

The Manor

Originally an "acre"—as its German equivalent *Morgen* still implies—must have been the area which could be ploughed with the implement and team of the time in one day, or rather in a long morning; in the afternoon the oxen which drew the ploughs would be driven to the pasture. But in England, as over a large part of western Europe, its shape came somehow to be fixed, at an early date, as that of a narrow rectangle, ten times as long as it was broad. The length was the length of a furrow, hence known as "a furlong"; and this was commonly forty times the measuring rod or pole. But for a long time there was great variety in the length of the local measuring rod; and it was only slowly that it came to be generally fixed at $5\frac{1}{2}$ times the small "clothyard." The breadth of the rectangle was four times the local measuring rod. Inasmuch as a strip forty rods long and one rod wide made up "a rood" (locally known very generally as "a land"), the acre may be described as four roods lying side by side. Yet we may fairly suppose that in stiff soils less ploughing would be got through in a morning than where the soil was lighter.

There is a further fact to be borne in mind. The great open fields, as we know them in mediæval and modern times, were broken up into a number of lesser units, each consisting of a group or, so to speak, a bundle, of acre or half-acre strips, all lying the same way and parallel to one another. These stretches of land were known as *shots, flats,* or still more commonly as *furlongs,* doubtless because they were a furrow-length in width. It may be that the expanse known as "a field" was consciously divided, at some time or

Economic Organisation

other, into these separate stretches (which were then further partitioned into parallel acre strips), in order to obtain as many such strips as possible by fitting them into the shape of the field. Or, as some conjecture, the furlong (in this sense), composed of a number of strips all lying the same way, may represent the piece of land freshly brought under cultivation, at some particular time, in a single (joint) undertaking; and thus the later great "fields" may be merely the result of the bringing into cultivation, one after the other, of several pieces of the waste lying in the same direction. But, whatever the origin of the arrangement may have been, it must have been much easier to make most of the acres of a uniform, comparatively narrow, width, than of a uniform, comparatively long, length. Accordingly it is in length rather than in width that the customary or nominal acres differed, by excess or defect, from the normal size. But whatever in each manor may have been called an acre, it was, as I have said, thirty of these acres that went, as a rule, to the yardland. With the holding of the whole or a fraction of a yardland went appurtenant and proportional rights of user in the common pasture and meadow. Where, as was commonly the case, the meadow was limited in area, the hay harvest was frequently apportioned among the tenants by lot or rotation; and similarly pasture rights, if "stinted" at all, depended on the size of the arable holding.

It should be added that the demesne itself was not apart from the common or open fields. It also was composed, more or less completely, of acre and half-acre strips, lying in the open fields, intermingled with

The Manor

the strips of the villeins. The gradual withdrawal of the demesne from the communal system and its consolidation in compact closes near the manor-house was one of those silent developments of the later centuries of the Middle Ages of which we know very little.

In order not to complicate the exposition, no mention has hitherto been made of the other classes that undoubtedly existed outside the villein-group. There were a certain number of "free-holders" and also of "socmen," who were tenants of the manor, but on conditions which were regarded as more "free" than those of villeins. There were also in some districts a dwindling number of persons who, whether called "slaves" or not, occupied an extremely servile position. The relations of these classes to the villagers proper or villeins is an exceedingly obscure subject; but it is pretty clear that, over a large part of the country, they were comparatively subordinate appendages to the manorial machinery. There was, however, a more important class, that of "cottars." These were perhaps as numerous as the villeins; and the compendious classification by Burns of the rural population of the Scotch lowlands, "the laird, the tenant, and the cottar," would have applied equally well to mediæval England. The cottars held, as a rule, but two or three acres of land—at most five; and probably many of them worked, for a large part of their time, for the more prosperous villeins. Historically, the class is of great interest; for it was certainly one of the chief sources from which has been derived the modern class of "agricultural labourers." But evidently the centre of the whole system was the

Economic Organisation

group of virgate-holders, or "yardlings"; and it is upon these that we are bound to concentrate our attention.

The status of the "yardling" and of the cottar beneath him is described with sufficient accuracy by the modern term "serfdom." The whole organisation of agriculture, that is to say the organisation of by far the larger part of the economic activity of the time, was, we may fairly say, based upon "serfdom." The word "serf" is, of course, a mere Englishing of the Latin word for slave, viz. *servus*. But "serfdom" means something very different from "slavery" to a modern ear, and quite properly. We mean by it a condition of dependence, in which the dependant was bound to the soil and subject to onerous burdens, but in which, whether technically "free" or not, he enjoyed an independent home life, and could not be sold away from his family and his holding; and in which, also, he possessed rights of property, at least in such movable wealth as he might acquire by his labour. This description is sufficiently applicable to the English peasant of the Middle Ages: even though we find it impossible to extract from contemporary lawyers, in any of the mediæval centuries, a definition of his status, in terms of freedom or unfreedom, which quite fits into the actual conditions of life. Understood as I have explained it, serfdom evidently occupies an intermediate position between slavery and freedom. All sweeping historical generalisations need large qualifications and exceptions to make them exactly accurate: historical evolution never moves quite regularly in any one direction: there are ups and downs, advances and re-

The Manor

trogressions. But, in a broad and general way, we may say that in the ancient classical world economic society rested on slavery. Slavery, we may recall, is taken for granted by Aristotle as a necessary constituent of a civilised community. And the modern world rests, formally at any rate and in theory, on individual liberty and freedom of contract. So that mediæval serfdom we may regard as representing, on the whole, an advance in social development.

But when we seek to go behind this generalisation, and to discover how, precisely, mediæval serfdom came into existence, we find ourselves at once in the midst of controversy. I began with the thirteenth century, because the abundant evidence from that period leaves us in little doubt as to the broad features of villeinage and of the manor as then constituted. And from that secure starting point, we can follow the subsequent development without troubling ourselves, unless we wish, with the question of origins. But I cannot leave so tremendous a problem without at least a few sentences of comment. I say "tremendous," because it is one that vitally concerns the whole of western and central Europe; and it has busily engaged continental historians, and especially German historians, as much as or even more than English. The distinction between the demesne and the rest of the "manor," "seigneurie," or "Rittergut"; the existence of a normal peasant holding, very commonly of some thirty acres; the week work of two or three days all through the year; the compulsory rotation of crops and fallow,—these were as universal and as uniform over the whole of western and central Europe as the theory of feudal tenure, or

Economic Organisation

the ideas of chivalry, or the constitution of the church: in eastern Germany they survived into the nineteenth century.

When serious attention was first turned to this subject, some sixty years ago, the creation of the manor and of its continental parallels was explained as due to the depression of village groups of freemen. One widely prevalent view made these supposed original freemen the corporate proprietors, as a body, of the land which they tilled, and regarded the later lord of the manor as taking the place of a preceding communal ownership. This was the form of the "primitive free man" view which was known as the "mark" or free village community theory; *mark* being a German term interpreted as the area owned by the group. But against this view it was urged that over large parts of Gaul the later seigneuries apparently grew, without any break of continuity, out of those estates of large proprietors, cultivated by semi-servile tenants, which we know to have existed in the later centuries of the Roman rule; and it might therefore be conjectured that its origin was directly, or indirectly by imitation, the same elsewhere. As such an estate was commonly called a *villa*, this may be briefly labelled "the villa theory." It was next pointed out that neither the Teutonic invaders of the Roman Empire, nor the Celtic peoples whom the Romans found in possession, and who may have survived, in greater or less proportion, after the Teutonic immigration, consisted entirely of free men: there were probably at least as many slaves as freemen among them. There are accordingly, for what is now England and France and

The Manor

western Germany, at least four possible groups of factors to be considered : (1) social conditions among the Celtic inhabitants, before and during the Roman rule ; (2) social conditions in the completely Romanised districts ; (3) social conditions among the Teutonic immigrants ; and (4) the forces at work within the new kingdoms of the west, between the period of the Barbarian invasions and the time when our evidence unmistakably shows us full-grown serfdom and manorialism. It is probably true to say that no historical scholar of to-day holds either the "mark" view or the "villa" view in an exclusive form. There is likely now to be pretty general agreement in the proposition that the Teutonic (including the Danish) invasions led to the settlement, over large parts of what is now England, of a considerable number of "common freemen," who settled down singly or in small groups to cultivate the land. On the other hand, it is tending to be recognised that the Roman agrarian system, the "villa" with its slaves or peasants bound to the soil, is not likely to have altogether disappeared in Gaul, and that it may even have survived in parts of Britain. In the process of manorialisation, which was a long one and occupied centuries, the example of the Roman serf-group may conceivably have had a large influence even in the districts which started, in the main, with a quite free population. We are, however, still a long way off the final and satisfactory adjustment, in an intelligible and convincing statement, of all the various elements which are clearly involved in the problem.

These elements may be summed up under two heads —communal and seigneurial. The communal features

Economic Organisation

of manorial life were all bound up with the system of intermixed holdings in the open fields: for that intermixture itself involved or led to a large amount of co-operation and common action. Because the holdings were intermixed, the several cultivators had to observe a common rotation of crops. For the same reason, and because of the absence of hedges or fences between the strips, the several tenants had to submit to the exercise by their fellows of certain "rights of common." The cattle of all the tenants must be turned out to graze freely over the stubble, as well as over the one great field whose turn it was to lie fallow that particular year. The common pasture or waste remained undivided, because for centuries it was too extensive to make it worth while to cut it up; and it was natural that men who were accustomed to act together in the cultivation of their acres should employ in common a village herdsman, shepherd, and swineherd. We may conjecture that the intermixture of holdings was originally designed to bring about a fair distribution of the land among all the occupiers, and to give each tenant his fair proportion of good and bad soil. And this purpose we may fairly suppose to have been very distinctly present to men's minds at a time when it was practically impossible to improve poor land. In the absence of artificial grasses there was little hay, and what there was was not supplemented by "roots." Accordingly there were few cattle, and these exceedingly puny; so that there was little manure available as fertiliser. We may conjecture further that the stripwise arrangement was the outcome, at some early period, of a system of co-operative ploughing; acre strips

The Manor

being naturally allotted to one member of the group after another because an acre was the extent of a day's ploughing. Evidence derived from Wales of a condition of things probably prior in development to the manor indicates that each of the villeins came to hold the same number of these scattered acres because each alike contributed a yoke of oxen to the eight-ox team. But why the acres should be of that shape; why thirty acres should be the common amount of holding; why the arable fields should so commonly be three—all these points are still obscure. How far they were due to free choice or imitation, going back to pre-manorial or "tribal" times, how much to coercion or pressure of some kind from above, has yet to be determined.

The seigneurial elements, on the other hand, were those specially bound up with the position of the lord of the manor: his authority over the land and those upon it: in particular the large share he possessed, under the name of demesne, of the tilled land (whether in separate closes or intermixed with the strips of his tenants), and his recognised right to exact labour services from his tenants as the necessary means of getting his demesne cultivated. It was in order to preserve undiminished the labour force upon the manor and tie it to the soil, that restrictions were put upon the personal freedom of the villeins; and it was in maintaining the due succession of able-bodied tenants and compelling them to render their accustomed services that that important part of the system which can only be barely alluded to here, the manorial court, found its most constant occupation.

Economic Organisation

It is clear that an open-field husbandry could have existed without any such division of the use of the land between lord and tenants as is found in the manor; and, on the other hand, that lords could have exercised a large authority, could indeed have exacted labour rents, even had there been no open-field system. This analysis of the manorial organisation may perhaps indicate the directions in which we shall have to look for a solution of the problem of its origin. In any case, it will be a help in following the history of its decline.

LECTURE II

The Stages of Industrial Evolution : the Gild as Starting Point

As, in tracing the history of the agricultural side of English life, I began with the thirteenth century in order to avoid controversy, so with the same object I shall begin an account of the manufacturing or industrial side with the fourteenth century. Long before that time a number of towns had firmly established themselves; and in those towns trade and manufacture were carried on to an extent considerable in itself, though still quite small in comparison with agricultural employment. And, towards the end of that century, the men who carried on the several industries were organised, in every town, in what it has become usual to speak of as "the gild system." Starting as late as this, I am compelled to omit much that is of extreme interest. The gild system, as I have already stated, was characteristic of industry in the towns; and indeed, with the exception of the arts of the village miller and the village blacksmith, and here and there a little mining and quarrying, all economic activity that was not directly agricultural was now, and for some time to come, centred in the towns. We ought, therefore, did time allow us, to deal with the tangled problem of the origin of the towns and of their constitution. The

Economic Organisation

growth of the towns means the appearance of non-feudal and non-agricultural forces in society; the rise of a non-servile middle class; the appearance of ideas of contract as opposed to custom, and of payment in money as contrasted with payment in kind or in service. And developments like these had a significance not limited to the towns; they exercised, as we shall see later, a slow but profoundly disintegrating influence on the feudal society of the "open country" around.

One would like, therefore, to point out the origin of many of our English towns in the needs of defence; the county town being the central fortress and garrison for the surrounding shire or county. The whole of the Midlands must, at some time or other, have been artificially cut up into sections — for "shire," like "section," means simply a piece shorn or cut off — and in the midst of each section was planted a stronghold. Other towns sprang up owing to the presence of the king's court, or the needs of a great cathedral or monastic establishment, or the great fairs at places of religious pilgrimage. I could like to enter into the question of the origin of the municipal constitution, whether in the manorial organisation or in market privileges, whether unconscious or conscious, gradual or rapid; and to consider how it was that the body of burgesses were able to acquire certain rights of self-government, and to establish their own municipal tribunals. And after insisting on specifically municipal characteristics, I should have to comment on the surprisingly agricultural character, after all, of many of the smaller towns down to a comparatively late period; so that the burgesses often continued to be almost as

The Gild System

much interested in open fields and rights of common as ordinary villagers.

All this, however, I have now to pass over. I can only just touch upon one development which was especially bound up with town life, and that is the beginnings of commerce as distinguished from manufacture. Earlier by a generation or more than the appearance of any numerous body of English craftsmen, a good deal of trading had sprung up in such native products as wool and woolfels, or in luxuries, such as fine cloth or silks or spices or wine imported from abroad. In every town the men who engaged in such trade were organised, as early as the twelfth and thirteenth centuries, in what were known as "merchant gilds." The one exception, curiously enough, was London. A document has indeed recently come to light which implies that in the capital also there was once a gild merchant. Yet the phrase here used is probably only the repetition of a current formula; and we have no other trace of the existence of such a body. But this was probably only because its objects were obtained there in other ways. The merchant gilds doubtless contributed largely to the formation of the mediæval municipal government; a trace of this influence remains in the common designation of the town hall in our older boroughs as the "guildhall." And the organisation of the merchant gilds probably served as a model for the earlier craft gilds. But the exact nature of the relations between the merchant gild and the craft gilds is still a subject of controversy; and I am reluctantly obliged to content myself with a bare allusion to a large and fascinating field of inquiry.

Economic Organisation

Craft "gild" and "gild system" have become the common modern terms for the industrial organisation of the later Middle Ages; and they are satisfactory enough if we understand just what they stand for, and realise that, in the sense in which we now use them, they are modern and not contemporary expressions. By the end of the fourteenth, or early in the fifteenth century, every occupation involving even a slight degree of skill gave rise to a systematic grouping of the men engaged in it; and a corporate organisation grew up, substantially similar in its main features in every industry and every town, which played a large part in the life of the time and was destined to exert a real influence for centuries later. But in the fourteenth and fifteenth centuries these groups were commonly known as "crafts," or, by a word of Anglo-French origin which had originally nothing "mysterious" about it, as "misteries" (French: *métiers*), which had precisely the same meaning. The "craft" or "mistery" of "cappers," or makers of caps, for instance, in fourteenth century speech, meant not only the skill of the cappers, but also and more immediately the group of cappers themselves, looked upon as a body possessing certain common rights and responsibilities, and capable of acting together.

As the fifteenth century went on, these bodies came more and more to be designated by the term that has clung to them ever since in London, viz. "companies." Some of them, like the companies of weavers in several towns, were, it is true, of very early origin, and dated from as far back as the first half of the twelfth century. These early craft bodies

The Gild System

had been actually known originally as "gilds," and kept the word as part of their official and formal title. But by the fifteenth century the word itself, as applied to craft companies, had passed out of popular use; and in the sixteenth it was applied, almost if not quite exclusively, to religious fraternities.

The controversy which has raged, and has not yet come to an end, as to the origin of the gild system, refers almost entirely to the earlier craft "gilds," actually so called. Their influence on the subsequent development has, I cannot help thinking, been somewhat exaggerated. By any one who looks dispassionately at the evidence of the fourteenth century, the appearance and universal extension of the craft organisation is seen to issue spontaneously out of the conditions of the time, and to require no explanation from earlier and obscurer periods. The gild system of the fourteenth and fifteenth centuries, speaking broadly and generally, was no result of a sudden uprising, of a class-conscious effort on the part of the craftsmen to secure autonomy, or even of a selfish striving after the gains of monopoly; it was the gradual and almost unconscious result of the coalescence of two groups of forces—forces from below, tending towards association and union, and forces from above, especially the pressure of the municipal government, tending towards corporate responsibility. Both these forces need some further explanation.

It was the universal practice for the men of each particular occupation in mediæval towns to live close together in the same quarter, practically monopolising particular streets and localities; this is sufficiently indi-

Economic Organisation

cated by the street names of our older towns. They therefore naturally attended the same parish churches. And just as rich individuals created endowments to provide for religious services on the anniversaries of their deaths, endowments known as "chantries," so it became the practice for the men of particular crafts, accustomed to stand or kneel in the same corner of their churches, to form "brotherhoods" or "fraternities" to provide for services on the occasion of the death of one of their number, or for the commemoration of all their departed on the festival of their patron saint. Such fraternities were simply religious clubs, and may be briefly described as "co-operative chantries" : in essence they were just like the numerous other religious brotherhoods formed by their side by other groups of men not all belonging to the same craft. It is easy to understand how a religious fraternity, when composed of most of the men of the town following a particular trade, would come to interest itself in purely trade affairs. It is not impossible that in some instances the fraternity was, from the first, a conscious veil for trade purposes ; but the main explanation of the fraternities within the crafts is to be found in the religious usages of the age and in local propinquity.

In an age which laid so much stress on the religious duty of almsgiving, these religious clubs would naturally assist their members in distress. Moreover, when the practice grew up of performing pageants or religious plays in the streets of the towns on certain great festivals of the Church, the craftsmen would, of course, desire to take a part. It became usual for the men of each craft to charge themselves, year after

The Gild System

year, with the performance of part of the sacred story ; if possible of that particular episode which was most akin to their own daily occupation. Thus the vintners would present the Marriage at Cana, the chandlers the Star in the East, and the shipwrights the Building of the Ark. Some of the "mistery plays," as they came to be called from being performed by misteries or crafts, have come down to us, such as those of York and Chester and Coventry. They are among the sources of the drama which flowered so rapidly under Elizabeth. And the long lists of the plays show how numerous were the occupations carried on in every town of any size.

But while these religious and social impulses were spontaneously drawing the several groups of craftsmen together, they were being made conscious of their community of interests in another and very different way. There was a strong public opinion in favour of protecting purchasers against fraudulent or defective workmanship. Occasionally, though perhaps not frequently, the men of a particular trade, finding that their craft was "badly put in slander," as it was said, by the roguery and falsehood of its members, themselves went to the town magistrates and asked for the appointment of authorised "overseers" or "assayers." But whether the men of the several misteries were desirous of regulation or no, the municipal authorities came to insist with more and more emphasis that there should be an adequate supervision, or, as it was then called, a "view," of every craft, in order to detect and punish "false" work. Accordingly we find group after group of

Economic Organisation

workmen admonished by the municipal authorities to choose from among themselves persons who should be responsible for the work and behaviour of their fellows. From time to time general directions were issued to the same effect, as in the following London ordinance :—

"It is ordained that all the misteries of the City of London shall be lawfully regulated and governed, each according to its nature in due manner, that so no knavery, false workmanship, or deceit shall be found in the said misteries, for the honour of the good folk of the said misteries and for the common profit of the people. And in each mistery there shall be chosen and sworn four or six, or more or less, according as the mistery shall need ; which persons, so chosen and sworn, shall have full power from the Mayor well and lawfully to do and to perform the same."

Being obliged in this way to come together and elect overseers or wardens, the crafts took the opportunity to draw up rules for the government of the trade. These rules were at first of the most modest character, and did little more than prescribe certain simple standards of honest workmanship. But they soon went on to regulate apprenticeship and admission to the trade. The "Articles," "Ordinances," or "Points" were then presented to the Mayor and Alderman for confirmation and enrolled in the municipal registers. The edifice was completed in the fifteenth century and subsequently by the acquisition of charters from the crown, definitely "incorporating" the bodies which had thus gradually and almost insensibly constituted themselves.

The Gild System

The history of the several trades shows very considerable divergencies between one craft and another, and between one town and another, and the separate institutional elements are hard to disentangle. In some cases, the craft, as such, provided for religious services and for the relief of sick or impoverished members. In other and more numerous instances, we can clearly trace the separate organisation of a religious fraternity within the industrial group, but apart from the trade machinery. But, in every case, both spontaneous tendencies towards religious and social co-operation and compulsory regulation by the municipalities contributed towards the creation of a sense of craft solidarity. And the result, by the middle of the fifteenth century, was a substantial uniformity both in craft organisation in all English towns, and in the municipal constitution which rested upon it. This uniformity, like the uniformity of the manorial system, extended to the whole of western Europe. The craft societies of London, Paris, Nuremberg, and Florence were fundamentally alike in form and functions; and the same is true, with necessary qualifications, of the smaller urban centres. The more backward countries of the north and east did, indeed, imitate their wealthier neighbours—Scotland following England, and Poland and eastern Germany following the Rhineland. But I do not know that there was much direct copying among the peoples of western Europe, nor do we need it to account for the facts. Apparently the same institutions everywhere grew up in much the same way, owing to the operation of the same causes. These causes were the uniform intellectual, social, and economic condi-

Economic Organisation

tions. Everywhere industry could only secure shelter and could only create a market in the towns; everywhere natural gregariousness drew the men of each craft together; everywhere public opinion demanded supervision and regulation; everywhere production was on a small scale; everywhere it was carried on in small workshops, by from one to four persons, without the aid of machinery; everywhere skill and reputation were more important than capital. The gild system would seem, indeed, to be a necessary stage in the development of industry; and the Chinese gilds of to-day show the ideas and machinery of the gilds of mediæval Europe still actively at work.

Much labour has been spent, and profitably spent, on the attempt to distinguish between stages in industrial evolution. I say profitably, because one of the best ways to penetrate into the essential characteristics of a particular state of affairs is to have some other state of affairs with which to compare it. We must take care not to allow our classification to become too rigid; but that ought not to be difficult. Allowance must be made for the possibility, and indeed the probability, of transitional and intermediate arrangements. And of course we must not suppose that every country, or even every occupation, must necessarily pass through all the several stages. New countries, like our own colonies, will naturally begin at the stage reached already in old countries, if the necessary conditions are present; and new industries, as we shall see later, like the cotton industry, will begin their career with the organisation which the contemporary but older

Stages of Industrial Evolution

industries have reached only after long centuries of development.

With these cautions we may roughly distinguish four stages in the history of industry during mediæval and modern times. It will be wiser for the present to leave the ancient world out of account.

First, there is that stage of affairs when there is no separate body of professional craftsmen at all; where all that can be called "industry," as distinguished from agriculture, is carried on within the household group, for the satisfaction of its own needs, by persons whose main business is the cultivation of the land or the care of flocks. The main activities of all except the fighting class are still in this stage preponderatingly agricultural; but the cultivators of the soil make their own clothes and furniture and utensils, and there is practically no outside "market" for their manufactures. It represents a long step in evolution when professional craftsmen come into existence: men who, though they may have small holdings of land which they cultivate, and may indeed receive their remuneration in the shape, to some extent, of these holdings, are yet primarily craftsmen—primarily, for instance, weavers or smiths. Such a specialisation alike of agriculture and industry affords one of the earliest and most striking examples of division of labour, and it brings with it some of the advantages which Adam Smith sets forth in his celebrated chapter. Production in this stage is still on a small scale; it takes place either at the customer's home or in a small workshop or room or shed within or adjoining the craftsman's own dwelling: and there is no intermediary between producer and customer.

Economic Organisation

The producer either works on the customer's own materials; or, if he buys his own material and has not only "labour" but a "commodity" to sell, he deals directly with a small neighbouring circle of patrons. There is a "market" in the modern business or economic sense, but it is a small and near one, and the producer is in direct touch with it; though, indeed, it may sometimes consist not of the ultimate consuming public, but of fellow artisans in some other mistery. The next stage is marked by the advent of various kinds of commercial middlemen, who act as intermediaries between the actual makers in their small domestic workshops and the final purchasers: the widening of the market being both the cause and the result of their appearance. And, finally, with the advent of costly machinery and production on a large scale, we have the condition of things to which we are accustomed in our modern factories and works, where the owners or controllers of capital not only find the market, but organise and regulate the actual processes of manufacture. To these several stages it is difficult to give brief designations which shall not be misleading. It is common to speak of them as (1) the *family* or *household system*, (2) the *gild* or *handicraft system*, (3) the *domestic system* or *house industry*, and (4) the *factory system*. But we can dispense with labels if we can remember the essential traits. Of the third and fourth we shall have much to say at a later point. For the present we have to do with the second, where there is a separate industrial class and a market or group of customers, though but a limited and local one. "Gild system" will indicate it accurately enough if we bear in mind

Stages of Industrial Evolution

that the gild was merely the form of organisation that was bound to be assumed under the conditions of the time, as soon as there came to be a number of professional craftsmen and these craftsmen were practically all collected in the towns.

Let us look now more closely into the company organisation. The craft company was not simply an association *among* men of a town engaged in a particular occupation; it was the association, in idea and approximately in fact, of *all* the men so engaged. That means that, as soon as the company was solidly established, no man who did not belong to it could carry on the trade in the borough. Compulsory membership was the necessary consequence not merely of self-interest but also of the public duties which were imposed upon the group; the representatives of the several trades could only be expected to be responsible for the good behaviour of those who had placed themselves under their authority. Compulsory membership is the same thing as monopoly. But—as this way of putting it implies—the character of such a monopoly depends on the ease or difficulty with which competent persons can secure admission. Undoubtedly in later centuries the craft companies used their privileges in the worst sense of monopoly. We all know, for instance, how in the middle of the eighteenth century James Watt was prevented by the Corporation of Hammermen from establishing himself as an instrument-maker within the town of Glasgow, and found refuge in the precincts of the University. But it does not seem that in the earlier periods of their history the craft companies were exclusive in any markedly harmful sense. Quite

Economic Organisation

early, indeed, they may have put obstacles in the way of men entering the occupation who came from other towns as adult craftsmen. But then in those periods there was, in fact, very little desire to move from one town to another.

Within the ranks of those occupied in the several industries there grew up in England, as elsewhere in western Europe, a sharp division into three orders. There were first the "masters," *i.e.* the full members of the society, who were authorised to set up shop on their own account. These were not necessarily masters in the modern sense, *i.e.* employers, since very many of them worked by themselves and employed no one. There were the "apprentices" (French: *apprentis*); boys and young men who were learning their trade, and whose term of service came to be generally fixed at seven years, in accordance with "the custom of London." This institution of a uniform and relatively long period of apprenticeship for all trades seems to be characteristic of England; certainly it was not found in France. And then there were the "journeymen," *i.e.* men paid by the day (French: *journée*), and not, like the apprentice, bound for a long period of indenture. Gradually the rule grew up that even to work as journeyman a man must have served a seven years' apprenticeship. It is the less necessary to dwell upon these distinctions, because the terms *apprentice* and *journeyman*, and the ideas associated with them, have survived in some occupations and places down to our own time, in spite of profound changes in the general situation. But it is perhaps well to make it quite clear that in none of

Stages of Industrial Evolution

the mediæval craft companies was there anything in the nature of a joint-stock or any associated trading on the part of the craft as a body. The nearest approach to it was the rule in some crafts that opportunities of buying material on advantageous terms were to be shared by all the members who cared to benefit by them. With this exception, the several masters were left free to carry on their trade each on his own stock and responsibility and for his individual profit: the gild authority " regulated "—to use a term prominent in a later age—individual enterprise, and did not replace it.

In the midst of the labour troubles of the nineteenth century there have been many who have looked back with regret to the gild system of the Middle Ages and have dreamt of its restoration. The gild system, as we shall learn later, was half destroyed in the sixteenth century by the advent of capital and the extension of the market, and its ruin was completed in the eighteenth by the introduction of machinery and, with it, of the factory system. Its restoration was economically impossible. Not only was this so: the admirers of the past have undoubtedly viewed the mediæval handicrafts in much too romantic, and even sentimental, a spirit. There was a good deal more selfishness about than is commonly allowed for, and more friction between the immediate interests of various classes and occupations. Yet no one can turn over the gild records from the fourteenth to the sixteenth centuries without seeing that a fair ideal did float in a vague sort of way before the more reflecting men of the time. This ideal we may sum up as the

Economic Organisation

maintenance of just and reasonable conditions of production and sale, in the interests alike of producers and consumers. The master craftsman combined, in many trades, the functions of the manufacturer with those of the merchant; or, if "merchant" be too fine a term, of the manufacturer with those of the dealer or shopkeeper. He bought his own materials, and his apprentice offered for sale to the public as they passed by in the street the goods made inside the shop, as Sir Walter Scott depicts in *The Fortunes of Nigel*. Of course there were some trades where, from the nature of the case, this was impossible, *e.g.* the building trades. The master craftsman, again, usually combined the functions of employer and skilled workman: when he employed apprentices or journeymen or both, he commonly worked by their side on the finer parts of the job, when not engaged with a customer. What the public desired, above everything else, was that the wares should be of good or standard quality. This was the main purpose of the whole system of regulation by gild wardens and town authorities. And many of the regulations which remind us of our modern humanitarian factory legislation, such as the prohibition of working at night, were designed, not in the interests primarily of the worker, but in the interest of the public; in order, that is, to facilitate the necessary supervision or to prevent a public nuisance. It does not seem that regulation extended, as a rule, to the determination of prices; but it was a fundamental article in the moral teaching of the church of the time, and in the opinion of the governing classes in the towns, that for every article

Stages of Industrial Evolution

there was a "just price," which ought neither to be fallen short of nor exceeded. And when there seemed to be need, as in the case of the bakers and innkeepers and vintners, to protect the public, the public authority did not hesitate to step in and enact a scale of prices not to be exceeded except under severe penalty.

As to entry into the trade: we must bear in mind that, throughout the Middle Ages, population was only very slowly expanding. So long as the industrial workers increased only in the same proportion as the general population, and did not outstrip the purchasing power of the community, the average apprentice might expect, as a general thing, after he had served his articles and had worked for a few years as a journeyman, to be able to set up for himself and to earn the kind of livelihood that was commonly felt to be appropriate to his class. Meanwhile the relations between employer and employed, within the small shops, were of a family or patriarchal character. We cannot say that there was in fact any complete and universal practice of fixing journeymen's wages by regulations of the gild or of the municipality. But that was simply because it was not found to be necessary. The principle, however, that wages should be just or reasonable—the belief that for each kind of labour there was some just or appropriate remuneration which could be ascertained, and, if need be, enforced—was as universally held as the principle of "just price," of which, indeed, it was but a part. And the craft authorities, with the approval of the municipalities, or the municipality alone when the craft was slow to act, did, as a matter of fact, inter-

Economic Organisation

vene and regulate the wages of journeymen in a good many particular instances.

Can we say that there already existed a "labour question"? That depends altogether on what we mean by "labour question." If we mean the problem how best to adjust the relations between a large number of persons who have only their labour to offer and a relatively small number of persons who employ them, in circumstances in which the successful carrying-on of production involves the presence of considerable quantities of capital of which the employers alone have the control—if that is what we mean by labour question, then, speaking broadly and generally, we may say it did not exist in the Middle Ages. But obviously in another sense it did exist, or existed in germ; for there must be a labour question, in a sense, as soon as one person comes to be employed by another. And in that sense, we may say that the gild system, so far and so long as it was true to its ideals, "solved the labour question."

But if, after stating these ideals, we turn to the actual history, and expect to find some well-marked epoch during which they were effectively realised, we are likely to meet with disappointment. The gild organisation itself was of slow and irregular formation. It was a long time before the necessity of apprenticeship, the sharp distinction between apprentice and journeyman, the regular election of wardens and the systematic supervision of processes, took quite clear and definite shape. And almost as soon as they did so, the little groups of masters began to show an inclination towards monopoly, and friction began to arise between them

Stages of Industrial Evolution

and the journeymen. Hardly, we are inclined to say, has the gild system been perfected before it begins to break down. It is perhaps more accurate to say that the gild ideals were in constant process of realisation and decay throughout the fourteenth, fifteenth, sixteenth, and even seventeenth centuries. And that is because of the width and variety of the field of their operation. New industries were growing, old industries decaying, and the smaller towns were constantly catching up with the larger ones and repeating their experience. Hence the spirit of monopoly might very well make its appearance in some gilds long before there was anything seriously at fault in others. In this sense, therefore—as a policy which, for varying periods in varying trades and varying towns, did actually succeed, to a large degree, in controlling industrial activity to the general satisfaction alike of the general public and of "the workers"—we may fairly say that the gild ideal was actually realised.

LECTURE III

The Beginnings of Modern Farming : the Break-up of the Manor

WE must now return to the condition of the agricultural population. It must be carefully borne in mind that, interesting as is the early development of manufactures and trade, England continued, until well into the eighteenth century, to be mainly an agricultural country; and the fortunes of its peasant cultivators form, until quite recent times, the centre of its economic history. We must concentrate our attention on the changes in the position of the yardlings and cottars, who constituted the bulk of the rural population. What we shall say will apply primarily to central and southern England; of the eastern counties and the western it will be true only with modifications.

The conditions under which most of the land was held by its peasant cultivators were, as we have seen, determined not by definite contract or bargain but by custom. They held indeed "in villeinage" or "in bondage," as the manorial records put it, but "according to the custom of the manor"; and while lawyers were perplexing themselves with the theory of their status, the essence of the real position of affairs is indicated by the introduction and spread of the term "customaries" or "customary tenants" as their everyday designation.

Beginnings of Modern Farming

Now mediæval "custom" is rather a deceptive thing: it is difficult to give it enough weight in our thoughts without giving it too much weight. On the one side there was certainly a strong and constant tendency to get into a groove; on the other hand changes were in actual fact made from time to time; and when once made, the new arrangement tended, in a curiously short time, to be itself regarded as of immemorial antiquity. And so we find that, though custom and habit were continually operating to keep things as they were, changes did take place—at first sporadically and slowly, and then generally and quickly—which profoundly modified the whole situation. For, by about the middle of the fifteenth century, that vitally important feature of the manorial system, the services of the customary tenants for the cultivation of the lord's demesne, had almost entirely passed away, and their place had been taken by money payments.

This is the largest and most widespreading and most significant example of the transition which has been conveniently expressed in German as a movement from *Naturalwirthschaft* to *Geldwirthschaft*. For this antithesis we have no satisfactory translation, for "natural economy" and "money economy" can hardly be called English; we can only more clumsily speak of a transition from a condition of things in which economic relations take the form of services and payments in kind to one in which they take the form of payments in money. But however we formulate it, the transition was of the utmost importance in the history of mankind. For it not only brought about, as we shall see in a moment, an

Economic Organisation

improvement in production; it prepared the way for the complete break-up of the old organisation. The use of a currency may indeed go on side by side for a long time with the dominance of custom: the force of usage may be so strong as to prevent, for an indefinite period, any modification of prices and wages which have once been arranged: but the inherent tendency of the use of a currency is to weaken custom. For it suggests valuation, in a way that the customary render of commodities or labour will never do. It prompts the inquiry whether a satisfactory value is being given or obtained; and accordingly it strengthens any disposition to change there may happen to be on either side of a connection.

The process of "commutation" of services for money is worthy of careful study, in relation both to its conditions and to its motives. The conditions were, first, that the manorial lord and manorial tenants should be familiarised with the idea of money payments. This was brought about by the extension of trade—first in the great fairs and in the towns, and then in the markets which sprang up during this period in every substantial village. It is significant that the earliest account rolls, drawn up by the bailiffs in charge of the demesnes, date from the middle of the thirteenth century. They show that the selling of produce and the hire of labour to supplement the villein services were becoming ordinary parts of a bailiff's work. Secondly, it required the actual existence of a sufficient and suitable metallic currency; such as was furnished by the issues and mint reforms of Henry III, Edward I, and Edward III. Thirdly, it needed a power on the part of

Beginnings of Modern Farming

the customary tenants to obtain some surplus produce from their fields over and above what was necessary for their own subsistence, which they could take for sale somewhere so as to obtain the coins to be offered to their lords. Fourthly, it involved the presence of a demand for this surplus produce, such as the towns were coming to furnish as their population grew beyond the resources of the fields just outside their own walls. The commutation of peasant dues for money is only explicable as the reflex result of a contemporary growth of industry and commerce. And, accordingly, it took place early in precisely those parts of western Europe where trade and town life first flourished. That it should take place early in England was due in the last resort to the causes which brought about an early growth of trade—not very considerable, perhaps, when compared with the Rhineland or the Netherlands or northern Italy, but considerable in comparison with central or eastern Europe. Among these causes are to be reckoned not only the physical advantages possessed by England, such as the abundance of harbours and navigable rivers, but even more the peace and order secured by the strong government of the Norman and Angevin kings.

So much, then, for the conditions or prerequisites of commutation. Now for its motives. Why did people want to pay money or to receive money instead of services? Much light is thrown on this problem by what happened in times much nearer our own in other parts of Europe. Labour services, precisely similar to those we have observed in England in the thirteenth century, continued to be rendered over a

Economic Organisation

large part of eastern Germany down to the later years of the eighteenth century, and in Poland, Hungary, and Russia down to the middle of the nineteenth. The effects of compulsory service (*Frohnden*) were observed and commented on by many an agricultural expert of the time. The opinion of all of them was that it exercised the worst possible influence upon production. This was most clearly evident in modern times to the landlords. A peasant who was called off from his own holding to work upon demesne land, in the produce of which he was not to share, was "naturally," said intelligent observers, a "reluctant labourer." "When long prescription has engendered a feeling that he is a co-proprietor, at least in the spot of land which he occupies, the reluctance to be called from the care of it to perform the task of forced work elsewhere is heightened by a vague sense of oppression, and he becomes dogged and sullen." It was alleged, with perhaps a certain exaggeration, that "in Austria in the eighteenth century the labour of a serf was equal to only one-third that of a free hired labourer." And though things were not so bad on the peasant's own holding, since there he had the stimulus of self-interest, the prior claim of the lord on two or three days of every week, and an additional claim just at those seasons, such as harvest time, when the tenant would be most anxious to get in his own crop, must have had a very depressing effect. It should, indeed, be remarked that the obligation did not always rest upon the tenant personally: his duty in England, at any rate in the fourteenth century, was defined, not as that of appearing himself, but as that of "finding a man to labour." Still,

Beginnings of Modern Farming

a great many peasants were probably so circumstanced that they had to furnish the labour with their own arms; and in any case the obligation would be an irksome and irritating one.

Such were the conditions and motives of commutation of labour obligations for money payments. And this commutation we can trace in England from its early and slow beginnings in the thirteenth century, through all its stages—"from the stage," as Maitland has put it, "in which the lord is beginning to take a penny or a halfpenny instead of each (day's) 'work' that in that particular year he does not happen to want, through the stage in which he habitually takes each year the same sum in respect of the same number of works, but has expressly reserved to himself the power of exacting the works in kind whenever he chooses, to the ultimate stage in which there is a distinct understanding that the tenant is to pay (a round sum as) rent instead of doing work." Or rather, I would add, to the final stage when not only the week work but the extra services or "boons" in harvest times and other busy seasons—which were long retained after the week work had been parted with—are all ultimately exchanged for cash.

Commutation was frequent but not general when the great Plague devastated the country in 1349, and returned, though with less virulence, in 1361 and 1369. In 1381 took place the Peasants' Revolt. The connection between Plague and Revolt is frequently misunderstood. A conjecture of Thorold Rogers in his earlier works became a confident assertion in his later, and was made the basis of William Morris' *Dream of John Ball*. It was to the effect that, com-

Economic Organisation

mutation having taken place, over the country generally, a generation or so before, and the Black Death having brought about a rise of wages, so that the commutation payments no longer purchased anything like the same amount of free labour, the lords of land sought to compel their tenants to return to labour rents, and thereby awakened an indignation which ultimately broke out in revolt. The revolt, in this view, was the reply of the tenants to an attempt of the lords of land to reverse the process of agrarian development. But for this view there is no evidence; and, besides, it implies that commutation had taken place on a much larger scale than we now know to have been the case. What happened was rather this. The Great Mortality made the tenants more conscious than before of the value to the lords of their services. Where—as was the usual case—the services had not yet been commuted for money, if the lord could not retain his tenants and their works he could not get his demesne cultivated at all. Made aware that they were indispensable, they began to press for the relaxation of their labour dues, or for the complete substitution for them of small round sums of money. But to such demands the landlords did not feel themselves in a position to accede. Free hired labour, as a result of the Black Death and the consequent dearth of available hands, had permanently risen in price some fifty per cent. This was in spite of the Proclamation which had been issued by the government directly after the Mortality and of the Statute passed in the next year, making it an offence to pay or demand more than the previously accustomed wage, and of the elaborate machinery of local "justices

Beginnings of Modern Farming

of labourers" which was called into existence to enforce the statute. The lords were likely, on the contrary, to cling only the more firmly to any labour still customably due; and where commutation was still recent, and the lord had expressly reserved to himself the option of labour,—which, as we have seen, was sometimes the case,—he would doubtless exercise it. And in their need for cash the lords would certainly use any decent opportunity that presented itself for getting ready money. Such an opportunity was given them by the manorial courts in which the tenants were bound to appear, and in which they could be fined for real or supposed breaches of duty. Under these circumstances the tenant peasants became more and more restive. This was the more natural because the doctrine of human equality was in the air. Popular preachers, chiefly of the Franciscan and Dominican orders, were going about asking:

> "When Adam dalf and Evë span
> Who was then the gentleman?"

Among such popular orators are certainly to be included Wyclif's "poor preachers." These were likely enough to make a very rough and ready use of their master's famous doctrine of "Dominion founded on Grace." All dominion or lordship, said Wyclif—and that included the authority of a manorial lord—was granted by God in return for service to Himself—that service which was involved in being in a state of grace. It was easy for the hearers of Wyclif's popular preachers to draw the conclusion that lords of land who refused to grant their demands could hardly be

Economic Organisation

in a state of grace, and that tenants were justified in refusing to carry out their usual obligations. Whatever the impulse, there is no doubt that a large number of the peasants did "withdraw their services"; and the coercive measures which followed led to the Revolt.

The Revolt brought about no sudden change; but in the years which closed the fourteenth century and during the early decades of the fifteenth, commutation went on much more rapidly than before, and that on terms favourable to the peasants; since it usually took place at the prices for the several works which had been customary before the Pestilence. And the reason was that, unless they consented to grant favourable terms, the lords could not keep their tenants; and, if the tenants went away, the lords would be left without either services or rent. The wholesale desertion of a village, at that stage of agrarian history, still involved, as for centuries before, the total destruction of the value of the estate; and, short of that, every single tenant lost and not replaced diminished its value proportionally. The situation was very different from what it came to be a century later. Then, as we shall find, the landlords were often only too glad to get rid of their customary tenants, because it left more scope for the extension of sheep-farming; and as this was a general movement on the landlords' part, a tenant who lost his holding in one manor was unlikely to find one elsewhere. But now the arrival in a village of a peasant willing to take up land would usually be welcome; so that a lord knew that, if he lost a tenant, some other lord would be glad enough to shelter him. Moreover, there was often room for newcomers in the

Beginnings of Modern Farming

growing industries of the towns : we learn of fugitive serfs who became tailors, shoemakers, weavers, and tanners. The outcome of the forces, not initiated but strengthened by the Pestilence, was, therefore, by about the middle of the fifteenth century, the practical disappearance, over the larger part of the country, of labour dues, and the substitution of money rents which soon, in their turn, became fixed by custom. This meant a heightened sense of personal dignity and independence on the part of the peasants, and the increased efficiency of all rural labour. And this latter improvement not only meant greater comfort to tenants and cottars ; it furnished, also, the food required by a growing urban population.

But of almost equal importance was another change that we find taking place. During the last half of the fourteenth century occasionally, and during the fifteenth century with greater frequency, we find it becoming the practice of manorial lords to let their demesnes for a short term of years, together with the rights and perquisites connected therewith, including the peasants' services or rents. Hitherto, so far as any individuals could be said to direct the traditional agriculture of the country, it was the lords of land who did so, personally or through their agents, their stewards and bailiffs. From this task, if it was a task, they begin now to extricate themselves, and the actual conduct of farming operations gradually passes out of their hands. The historical significance of this development was obscured to us until recently by our having forgotten the sharp and clear distinction in the typical manor between the demesne on the one side and the

Economic Organisation

villein or customary land on the other. A fixed payment in lieu of varying receipts or profits was known in the Middle Ages as a "ferm" (Latin: *firma*); and the lessee of a demesne for a term of years was accordingly known as a "firmar," "fermor," or "farmer." In the fifteenth or sixteenth century we may say with some confidence that "farmer," when used in an agricultural sense, most commonly meant a person who had taken on lease a demesne or part of a demesne; it was much later that it was extended to include every person in charge, on his own account, of an agricultural holding. Now, as we have already said, the characteristic of English agriculture in recent centuries has been the position of the capitalist farmer—the man cultivating as tenant a relatively large holding and himself supplying at least that part of agricultural capital that is necessary for the ownership of the stock and farming implements and for the payment of his labourers. In the farmers of the demesnes in the fourteenth, fifteenth, and sixteenth centuries we find one of the chief historical sources of the modern farmer class. But they differed at first from modern farmers in that they did not possess anything like so much capital. And the reason was that they were often men who had themselves acted as bailiff or reeve of the manor. Now that, with the increase of wages, the cultivation of the demesne had become much less profitable, it might naturally seem that a man on the spot, who had the incentive of personal interest and a minute knowledge of the capacities of the land, could make more out of it. Some such enterprising reeves might be relatively well-to-do: the reeve described by Chaucer

Beginnings of Modern Farming

was a better business man than his lord, had quickly put together a little capital ("ful riche he was a-stored pryvely!"), and knew how to get his lord's thanks by lending him what was really his own. But few such men could at once find the stock required for so large a holding as a whole demesne; and it was the most natural thing in the world that at first the lord's stock on the demesne should be let with the land itself and the other appurtenances. Such an arrangement seems to have gone on and the lease been renewed from time to time for about half a century after the plan had been adopted on any particular estate. This suggests that in about fifty years the farmers of the demesne lands usually managed to acquire sufficient capital to buy their own stock. By that time, also, the larger demesnes were probably getting broken up into smaller holdings, which would not call for so large a capital.

It is to Thorold Rogers that we owe our knowledge of this stage in English agrarian evolution. He realised that "farming capital," of which we are accustomed to speak so easily as a thing that explains itself, requires to be historically accounted for; and he perceived that what he called "land and stock leases" furnished the earliest opportunities for its creation. But his comparison of such a lease with the *métayer* system of the Continent has proved misleading. With that system the only feature it had in common was the provision of stock by the landlord; and under the *métayer* plan even that was neither universal nor uniform. The "farmer" of the English Middle Ages contracted for a fixed money rent; the essential feature of *métayer* tenancy is the payment to the landlord

Economic Organisation

of an agreed or customary proportion of the produce, commonly a half (whence, indeed, the name). Moreover, the English "farmer's" holding was from the first comparatively large; that of the *métayer* has almost universally been small. The former, in fact, replaced the lord on the demesne; the latter developed out of (or occupied the place of) the small, villein, tenant. And close as may seem the connection between giving the landlord half of the serf's produce and giving half of the serf's working week (whichever may be the earlier), I know of no evidence for a *métayer* stage in this country.

In the second half of the fifteenth century began a movement altogether different from anything that had been seen before. Since the advent of skilled weavers from the Low Countries in the reign of Edward III, England had ceased to be dependent upon the Continent for its supply of the better sorts of woollen cloth, and the manufacture had begun to grow with rapidity. This caused a more widespread demand for wool; and as hired labour continued to be dear, and pasture farming required far fewer hands than tillage, a movement began in the direction of sheep-farming, which soon went far to change the face of the country. For the keeping of sheep involved the fencing of the lands on which they were turned out to feed; and as those lands, whether tilled fields or pastures, had hitherto lain open, the process became known as "enclosure." In some counties there was plenty of stone at hand wherewith to build walls; but in the centre and south of the country no stone was easily obtainable, and the enclosures took the form of hedges. And

Break-up of the Manor

it was then that rural England began to acquire its present aspect.

Now the introduction of sheep might be the work of several different sets of people—of small freeholders, or even of the larger customary tenants; but our evidence makes it clear that it was chiefly the work of the manorial lords. Again it might take place on different parts of a manor: if it took place on the common pasture it might possibly hamper the tenants in the enjoyment of their own customary rights, but do no more. But, under the circumstances of the time, it could hardly take place on a large scale without encroaching on the arable fields. These usually stretched for hundreds of acres immediately around every village; and if they had to be left undisturbed, the remaining available land would often be insufficient and difficult of access. Many of the acres scattered up and down the open fields still in many places belonged to the lord's demesne; in earlier times, as we have already seen, the bulk or even the whole of the demesne had lain intermixed with the yardlands of the tenants in the open fields. By the middle of the fifteenth century the lords had succeeded, in large measure, in disentangling their demesne from the open fields and getting it together in compact areas. If a lord so placed chose to use his enclosed demesne for sheep rather than for crops, he could please himself and injure none except the cottars whom he no longer needed to employ, or the tenant to whom he may previously have let part of it. But where the demesne still lay in the open fields, the lord could do nothing with separate acre or half-acre strips: to be able to enclose spaces of convenient size he must somehow

Economic Organisation

get into his hands the adjacent strips of his tenants. For this and other reasons, we find that enclosure very commonly meant, in practice, the disappearance of a number of customary holdings in the open fields. It was now that the process started which I began by saying we should find one of our main subjects of attention in English economic history—viz. the removal from the land of that class of small peasant cultivators which is still so conspicuously attached to it in France and Germany.

The legal character of the changes in question has been the subject of much discussion, and cannot even yet be said to be satisfactorily determined. My own opinion is that they were greatly facilitated, in the earlier stages of the enclosure movement, by the uncertain state of the law as to customary tenancy. The villeins of the thirteenth century were technically said to hold " at the will of the lord, according to the custom of the manor." In the course of time the second half of the clause had come to be understood as limiting the first half : so long as a tenant performed his customary services, the general feeling was that he should not be disturbed. In not a few cases, indeed, it had come to be the practice, when a new tenant was being admitted, to make the grant expressly one " for life." Where that had been done, a lord who wanted to resume such a tenement had but to wait till the occupier died. It was certainly the custom, even when the tenancy was distinctly for life, to admit the son of the last holder ; but evidently in this case no legal claim could be put forward and the custom could be disregarded. Where no

Break-up of the Manor

such limitation to a life or lives had been expressed in the admission of the tenant, the next heir might seem to be safe in his appeal to custom when he sought admission. But the lord had a recognised right to receive a "fine," or payment on admittance. It was generally recognised that the fine should be "reasonable." But it was not till far in the reign of Elizabeth that this principle received judicial confirmation, and still later that the reasonable fine was fixed at twice the rental. It is highly probable that in many cases the lords got holdings back into their hands by the simple plan of demanding an impossible fine. But we can go still further : there is a good deal of evidence that, in the earlier years of the movement, a certain amount of actual eviction took place of sitting tenants. Listen to the account given in his *Utopia* by Sir Thomas More in 1516. He has been explaining, through the mouth of an imaginary foreign observer, how it was that there were so many thieves in England. After mentioning causes common to England and the Continent, he goes on : "There is another cause which, as I suppose, is peculiar to you Englishmen alone. . . . Your sheep, that were wont to be so meek and tame and so small eaters, be become so great devourers and so wild that they eat up and swallow down the very men themselves. . . . For look in what parts of the realm doth grow the finest and dearest wool, there noblemen and gentlemen, yea and certain abbots . . . leave no ground for tillage; they enclose all into pastures : they throw down houses, they pluck down towns," *i.e.* villages, "and leave nothing standing, but only the church to

Economic Organisation

be made a sheephouse. . . . That one covetous cormorant . . . may compass about and enclose many thousand acres of ground together within one pale or hedge, *the husbandmen be thrust out of their own,* or else either by covin and fraud or by violent oppression they be put beside it, or by wrongs and injuries they be so wearied that they be compelled to sell all. By one means, therefore, or another, either by hook or crook, they must needs depart away. . . . Away they trudge, I say, out of their known and accustomed houses, finding no place to rest in." We must not suppose, because this description of the England of his own time was prefixed by way of a foil to his account of the happy state of Utopia, that More was a mere literary idealist. He was a trained lawyer and administrator: seven years later he became Speaker of the House of Commons, thirteen years after, Lord Chancellor. The language in the next reign of Bernard Gilpin, the model parish priest, is to a like effect. Speaking of certain landlords, "for turning poor men out of their holds," he says, "they take it for no offence; but say the land is their own." The same conclusion is forced upon us by the evidence given before Royal Commissioners in 1517 of wholesale enclosures here and there: three hundred acres in one place and three hundred in another, with the refrain in each case "and the inhabitants have departed." Nay, in one case, that of Stretton Baskerville in Warwickshire, where "twelve messuages and four cottages" were "decayed," and six hundred and forty acres of land enclosed, "so that eighty persons there inhabiting were constrained to

Break-up of the Manor

depart thence and live miserably," the clearance seems to have taken place all on one day, which almost a quarter of a century later the people of the district remembered to have been the sixth day of December in the ninth year of Henry the Seventh.

At a later time, it is true, the "tenant by custom" was protected by the king's courts. Brian, Chief Justice, is reported as saying as early as 1481 that "his opinion hath always been and ever shall be that if a tenant by custom paying his services be ejected by the lord, he shall have an action of trespass against him"; and by 1530 this dictum got into the standard legal text-book. It is highly probable, however, that when the enclosure movement began, the national law courts were only just beginning tentatively to recognise a right of property in the customary tenant, and that many a man was ejected who, even half a century later, would have had too well recognised a right to his holding to be disturbed.

At some period not yet quite satisfactorily determined, customary tenants came to be known as "copyhold" tenants, since they were said to hold by copy of the court roll on which their services were registered. And undoubtedly copyholders have been secure in their holdings from the early part of the seventeenth century. "Now," wrote Sir Edward Coke, the great authority on the common law in the reign of the first Stuart, in a special little treatise on the subject, "copyholders stand upon a sure ground; now they weigh not their lord's displeasure; they shake not at every sudden blast of wind; they eat, drink, and sleep securely; only having a special care

Economic Organisation

of the main chance, to perform carefully what duties and services soever their tenure doth exact and custom doth require : then let the lord frown, the copyholder cares not, knowing himself safe and not within any danger. For if the lord's anger grew to expulsion, the law has provided several weapons of remedy; for it is at his election either to sue a *subpœna* or an action of trespass against the lord. Time hath dealt very favourably with copyholders in divers respects." Recent investigations have begun to show us how this security was probably established by the action of the royal courts in the fifteenth and sixteenth centuries. But these investigations have also shown us that time and the courts "dealt favourably with copyholders" by a sort of winnowing process. The term "copyholder" was apparently, for some time, applied very loosely to almost any kind of customary tenant, including even tenants for life or lives. But it was only "copyholders of inheritance," as the favoured class came to be called—holders of "good and perfect copyhold lands," as another contemporary phrase described them—who could appeal to the king's courts with any confidence. Some figures recently published go to show that when the courts did begin to bestir themselves, there were about as many manors in which copyholders were understood to have no "estate of inheritance" as there were in which they were more fortunate.

But whatever the legal character of the change may have been in any particular case, the economic effect was the same. In the language of Lord Chancellor Bacon—looking back on the changes which began

Break-up of the Manor

indeed a century before his time, but had continued to be warmly discussed—"arable land was turned into pasture; and tenancies for years, lives and at will, whereupon much of the yeomanry lived, were turned into demesnes," *i.e.* were brought into the lord's own possession.

Loud complaints about enclosures from writers of every class abound in our sixteenth-century literature: they seem to indicate an agrarian revolution; and we know that they caused the gravest concern to our statesmen, and called forth repeated legislative acts and strong assertions of executive authority. To these we shall return. Yet certain recent writers have urged, with a good deal of apparent force, that the transformation actually effected was nothing like as great as has been commonly supposed. Basing their conclusions upon certain contemporary evidence before royal commissions, they have shown pretty conclusively that in this first period—from, say, 1450 to 1610—enclosures were confined mainly to the midland group of counties: Leicester, Northampton, Rutland, Warwick, Bedford, Berks, Bucks, Oxford, and Middlesex. But when they go on to reckon that even in these counties less than one-tenth of the soil was affected, they seem to press their evidence beyond what it will bear, and to forget certain important considerations. My own minimum estimate for the above-named counties would be that about one-fifth of the arable land was affected; and this was certainly quite enough to occasion considerable alarm. Moreover this estimate does not include the *demesne* land laid down to pasturage; great distress might be

Economic Organisation

caused thereby among the cottars who had previously lived chiefly by wages, and now had to abandon their cottages and patches of land and move elsewhere, even though no "yardling" or "half-yardling" families were disturbed in their holdings.

All the developments we have been following—the transformation of labour-rendering into rent-paying customary tenants, the removal of many of the customary tenants in consequence of enclosures and the introduction of sheep-breeding in the place of tillage, the growth of a class of large "farmers" on the demesnes, gradually accumulating their own farming capital—all these had new and greater consequences at the time of the Reformation. The Reformation in religion, whether for good or for ill, was an expression of individualism; it emphasized the direct relation to God of the individual soul. But religious individualism was but a part or aspect of a universal tendency in the direction of freeing the individual from tradition and usage and stimulating him to think and act for himself. And this took shapes both good and bad: it showed itself in greater individual enterprise and improved methods of production, and it showed itself in more obvious selfishness and self-seeking; what contemporary writers call "private affection," "private profit" and "singular lucre." In all the economic relations of human beings with one another, it meant more of what we now call "competition," with all that it involves.

Now it would be absurd to depict the earlier centuries as a time when self-seeking did not exist. But there can hardly be any doubt that in the sixteenth century

Break-up of the Manor

self-seeking became more general, more alert, more unabashed; and of course this manifested itself very clearly in men's relations to land, which was still the basis of national life. English land even to-day—if we compare our prevailing practices and feelings with those current in America or Canada or Australia—is only partially commercialised. Men do not in England, even yet, commonly think of land as a source of profit exactly in the same way as they think of a cotton mill; and English economists still prefer to distinguish "land" pretty sharply from "capital." Yet English land, though not completely, is largely commercialised: and it was in the period of the Reformation that this commercialisation first made headway. "Farms," for instance (*i.e.* farms of demesnes or portions of demesnes), came to be looked upon as sources of profit; would-be tenants came forward to offer higher rents, or to buy the reversion when the term of the sitting tenant should expire. Money made in trade in the towns turned in this direction for investment, and city business men competed for farms with countrymen. Landlords naturally took advantage of the opportunity to increase their incomes, and were roundly abused by the preachers and pamphleteers of the time as "rent raisers" and "rent enhancers." Bishop Latimer declared in one of his sermons that for a farm for which his yeoman father had paid a rent of three or four pounds by the year, his successor was now paying sixteen pounds or more; and in another place, referring to farms on a larger scale, that "that which heretofore went for twenty or forty pounds by the year is now let for fifty or a hundred pounds by the year."

Economic Organisation

And an additional impulse and excuse was given by the rise of prices which followed upon the debasement of the currency in the later years of Henry VIII and under Edward VI.

To the new feeling concerning land a greatly wider scope was inevitably given by the dissolution of the monasteries in 1536 and 1539. It has been reckoned that about one-fifth of the land of the country now passed, by gift or easy terms of sale by the crown, into the hands of lay lords and gentry, in addition to whatever they held before. "Those families," wrote Hallam in 1827, "within and without the peerage, which are now deemed the most considerable, will be found, with no great number of exceptions, to have first become conspicuous under the Tudor line of kings; and, if we could trace the titles of their estates, to have acquired no small portion of them, mediately or immediately, from monastic or other ecclesiastical foundations." This is true not only of several of the great Whig houses of the eighteenth century, "the great civil and religious liberty families," of whom Disraeli gives the typical history in *Sybil;* it is true also of many of the substantial country gentlemen, like the family to which Oliver Cromwell belonged, who formed the strength of the Puritan and parliamentarian party in the seventeenth century. It is not my business here to discuss the question whether or no this was the best disposition of the wealth of the monasteries under the circumstances of the time and in the interests of the future; it is sufficient to call attention to the facts themselves. Of the suppressed smaller monasteries the number is said to have been three hundred and seventy-six; of the

Break-up of the Manor

greater, probably about two hundred and fifty; some six hundred and twenty-six in all. Probably in at least five hundred parishes the dissolution involved the substitution of a layman for an ecclesiastical body in the ownership of the whole or a considerable part of the manor. Now it is the universal experience—not in England only—that ecclesiastical and similar corporate bodies are conservative in their policy and easy-going in their demands. The rentals paid to the monasteries by the farmers of demesne land and the fines on renewal paid by the customary tenants were probably, as a rule, relatively low. But now came the new owners, moved by the new spirit of gain. They enhanced rents, converted in many places arable into pasture, and tried to bully customary tenants to accept leases for lives or periods of years. We must not exaggerate the extent of these changes; after a period of disturbance, the new owners settled down on their estates, and rents—having been adjusted to the new conditions of agriculture and the new range of prices—tended once more to become stationary. Moreover very many customary tenants did survive under the new name of "copyholders," with a legal security of tenure. Even the open field, with its compulsory rotation, remained over the larger part of rural England, though in a less complete and symmetrical form. Still the beginnings had been made of the new system of capitalist farming; and many of the peasant cultivators had disappeared from the land.

LECTURE IV

The Rise of Foreign Trade: the Advent of Capital and Investment.

IN turning now to consider the beginnings of England's foreign trade, we must steadily bear in mind that, though the interest of the subject is great, both for the light it casts on the conditions of the time and also because of the dominant part which foreign trade was destined ultimately to play in English development, its bulk was relatively very small throughout the Middle Ages, in comparison with the total economic activity of the nation. England remained on the whole a self-sufficing country: export carried away only such surplus raw produce as the land did not itself require, especially wool; and import brought chiefly luxuries, such as silks, furs, fine and dyed woollen cloth, and French wines, purchased by a very limited upper class, together with the spices which rendered more palatable the food and drink of the well-to-do. Probably the only imported article in general use among the masses of the people was the Norwegian tar which was employed as dressing for sheep in cases of scab: this seems to have been introduced at the end of the thirteenth century. Down to the close of the Middle Ages, England was far inferior to certain other parts

Foreign Trade

of Europe,—to the Rhineland and the great cities of north and south Germany on the one side, to the Italian republics, such as Genoa and Venice, on the other,—in manufacturing skill, in accumulated capital, in commercial enterprise, in knowledge of the arts of navigation and of accounting, and in the possession of shipping. It was really only in the seventeenth century that England began to compete with the other nations of western Europe on anything like equal terms, and only in the eighteenth century that it took the place of Holland and became the great carrying and entrepôt nation of the world.

I shall group what I have to say on this subject around two problems, which were closely connected. When our story begins, the foreign trade of England may be described as of the "passive" kind. Imports were brought to our shores almost exclusively in foreign ships by foreign merchants, and exports were carried away in foreign ships by foreign merchants. It was a position of affairs similar to what exists in China to-day and existed even in Russia a century ago. Chinese goods hardly come to Europe on Chinese ships at all; as late as the middle of last century Russian merchants only conducted one-ninth of the import and one-forty-fourth of the export trade of their own land. From a position like this we have to see how English foreign trade became "active," and how not only the distribution of imports and the collection of exports within the land, but the undertaking of the actual business of import and export was assumed by English hands. The second problem is the organisation of this new branch of activity, its relation to the form of

Economic Organisation

organisation that had already grown up for internal trade and industry, and the gradual development of new forms to meet the peculiar needs of foreign undertakings.

To begin, then, with the state of affairs when our foreign trade was practically entirely in the hands of foreigners. In some respects foreignness may be said to have had nothing to do with nationality; and in strictness I ought rather to speak of "alien" merchants when I mean merchants from other countries. For in the thirteenth and fourteenth centuries, "foreigner" (from *forinsecus*) meant simply an outsider, a man from a distance: it was applied as freely to a man from another town in the same country as to a man from another country; and in some important aspects all "foreigners," whether aliens or not, were treated alike by the townsmen to whom they came. They were welcome so far as they gave business to the resident burgesses of the towns to which they came: so far, that is, as they brought things which the burgesses could sell for them, or took away goods which the burgesses could buy for them. But they were most unwelcome when they tried to deal directly with non-burgesses or to sell retail. For the conception of a "national" trade was only beginning to grow up; and the unit of commercial life was still the town and not the nation. Of course foreigners who were also aliens were doubly foreign: their speech bewrayed them. And at a time when law was not yet completely "territorial" but was still largely "personal"; when, that is to say, a man, wherever he might travel, was thought to have a right to be tried by the laws to which he had been

Foreign Trade

accustomed, it was inevitable that alien merchants in England—a country still relatively barbarous—should live a somewhat separate life. They were very much in the position of the communities of European merchants until recently in China. Like them, they were restricted to a few ports and trading centres, and not allowed to penetrate freely into the interior. And they were watched with anxious concern to see that they did not defraud the simple-minded native burgess, or invade his monopoly either of the collecting or of the distributing trade in the country itself.

Particular bodies of foreign merchants were able to purchase for themselves valuable trading privileges and to secure the right to trade with England on paying only moderate duties. Of these the most important were the German merchants known as the Teutonic Hanse, and the merchants of Italy, above all those of Venice. The Teutonic Hanse was a great confederation of German towns, inspired throughout by what were conceived to be the interests of their traders. "To navigate is a necessity for us, to live is not" (*Navigare necesse est: vivere non est necesse*), was its proud motto. In its earlier history its leader was Cologne, owing especially to its eminence in the manufacture of cloth; later the Baltic towns, led by Lübeck, came to the front, owing to the immense importance of the herring fisheries which they then controlled. Some one has rather bitterly said that the herring and the clove (the chief object of Eastern trade) have caused more bloodshed than anything else except the Christian religion. Into the historical importance of the herring I cannot here enter. Suffice it to say that, during the

Economic Organisation

fourteenth century, the Hanseatic towns, banded together in opposition to the Danish monarch who sought to control the entrance to the Sound, grew into something very much like a federal republic; though each of the city-states which constituted it was subject nominally to the Emperor, and many of them also to some nearer territorial prince. Of the settlements of their merchants in foreign countries, the most important were the four "counters" at Bruges, Bergen, Novgorod, and London: in the last-named city they possessed a settlement, surrounded by a strong wall and comprising warehouses, residences, a fine hall and a pleasant garden, which was known as the Steelyard, and which occupied a site on the Thames bank now taken by Cannon Street railway station. At first practically the whole trade between England and Germany was in their hands; to the end of the sixteenth century they succeeded in excluding Englishmen from entering into direct commercial relations with north Germany and the Baltic. They always paid export duties lower than other aliens, and usually somewhat less than were paid by Englishmen themselves. In the relations of international trade, the Steelyard served much the same purpose as the famous settlement of South German merchants in Venice known as the Fondaco dei Tedeschi, with this important difference, that the Italian republic was not in the earlier and more primitive stage of commercial development still occupied by England. Perhaps a closer analogy may be found in the mediæval "factories" of the Italian merchants in the Near East, and of the English East India Company later in the Far East.

Foreign Trade

Equally characteristic of the time were the privileges and tariff preferences granted by the English government to Venice for the benefit of her merchants. After various experimental arrangements earlier in the fourteenth century, intercourse between the two states settled down in its closing years into a regular system which survived well into the sixteenth century. Every year Venice despatched a great fleet of galleys, with Bruges, the busiest centre of the trade of western Europe, as its ultimate destination. These " Flanders galleys," as they were called, visited on their way Syracuse, Majorca and the ports of Spain and Portugal, and then struck north for the English Channel. A part of the fleet usually turned off to Southampton, while the rest went on to the Low Countries. Arrived at Southampton, the Venetian traders remained doing business for several weeks, until it was time to rejoin their consorts and return home. The fleet, be it observed, was a public undertaking. The ships belonged to the state of Venice, which appointed the commander of the whole flotilla and provided captains and crews and fighting men. The right of freighting a ship was put up to auction; and though the trading was all done by individual merchants or small partnerships, and there was no general joint-stock, the character of the cargoes and the places and periods of trade were all carefully regulated by the government, and no one was allowed to send goods to England except in this annual fleet. No doubt the rulers of Venice, who were themselves merchants, were right in thinking that it was very expedient to keep their ships and men together: in this way they could provide the more

Economic Organisation

completely for their safety, maintain stricter discipline and a higher standard of commercial morality, and make better terms with the several foreign governments. The policy of the Venetian government was precisely similar to that of the Hanse : it was directed to two ends : to securing a good market in England and the Low Countries for the commodities, both of home production and obtained from the East, in which they traded, and to gaining all the profit that could be derived from their position as the sole source of supply for Mediterranean countries of English, French, and Flemish commodities. All outsiders, including the citizens of the countries where they themselves enjoyed large privileges, were absolutely excluded from the whole of the Mediterranean under their control.

But, obviously, such one-sided arrangements as these with the Hanse and Venice could not permanently survive when a number of Englishmen made their appearance, anxious and capable themselves to take part in foreign trade. The remarkable thing is that the privileges of the foreigners were retained by them so long after well-organised bodies of English rivals had begun to call their monopoly in question.

The first of these were the so-called Merchants of the Staple or Staplers. By "staple" was understood a fixed or appointed market. From quite early in the fourteenth century it was the settled policy of the English government to appoint certain fixed places at which all sales of wool, the chief product of the country, should take place, and to which accordingly all English merchants who dealt in wool were bound to resort. The frequent changes of location—some-

Foreign Trade

times one, sometimes several, places in England itself being chosen for the staple, sometimes a place on the Continent, usually Bruges—give an appearance of vacillation to the policy which does not really belong to it. The policy itself was throughout consistent: it was to mark out regular channels through which the stream of trade should flow, so that it might with facility be both protected and taxed. At last the choice of the government fixed permanently upon Calais, which combined the advantages of a continental situation with those of English rule; and there the staple for wool remained for a century and a half—from 1399 until the town was lost to England in 1558.

We can discern the gradual consolidation of the group of English wool-staplers into a definite organisation—the Mayor and Company of the Staple—on exactly the same lines as the craft companies. Like the craft companies, it resulted from the conjunction of two forces—the impulse towards fellowship spontaneously felt by men engaged in the same business, men having the same interests and running the same risks, and the need of regulation and control felt by the government, partly for fiscal reasons, but partly, also, from an honest desire to safeguard national interests. And this body necessarily, under the circumstances of the time, enjoyed a monopoly as against other Englishmen. Whether this monopoly was in practice irksome would depend upon whether it was exercised in an exclusive spirit, and whether there really were any number, worth speaking of, of competent merchants excluded from member-

Economic Organisation

ship. These questions we do right probably in answering, for the earlier part of the company's history, in the negative.

We might have supposed that a body of Englishmen engaged in the export of wool would have speedily come into conflict with the privileges of the foreign merchants, since wool was the main export article of the "Hansards" and a chief export article of the Italians. But the staplers were limited by their own government to Calais: from Calais, through the foreign merchants who resorted thither to meet them, they were able apparently to supply a considerable market in the Netherlands and the north of France; and this seems on the whole to have satisfied them.

Far different was the state of mind of a younger English body of traders, the Company of Merchant Adventurers. Their very name indicates the conscious growth of a new spirit among Englishmen. These merchants aimed at going further afield and engaging in foreign trade across the seas outside the limits of English territory; they aimed also at finding a market abroad for the new manufactured commodity which England was beginning to produce on a large scale, viz. woollen cloth. In both these ways they were looked upon as peculiarly enterprising and as undertaking a distinctly greater risk or "adventure" than the staplers. True, the gregariousness and sense of common interest even among these Adventurers was so strong that they too soon began to form themselves into a company, organised like one of the great city companies of London. Moreover, though the whole

Foreign Trade

world was before them, the foreign market into which they really 'desired to press was just the other side of the Channel and the North Sea. And there they were forced, if not by governmental regulation by the circumstances of the time, to make some one particular town their "staple," and establish themselves in an imposing and commodious House. They could not get the right of settlement or the right to trade—which alone made settlement worth while—except by a licence from the local prince; they could only offer attractive terms to a foreign prince by agreeing to come together at some one place; and only in this way, also, could they protect their common interests when the settlement had taken place. They naturally sought first to establish themselves at Bruges, the then centre of the trade of western Europe. But Bruges was itself a seat of the manufacture of cloth, and was allied to Ghent which carried on that manufacture on a still larger scale. On their famous woollen cloth rested the prosperity of all the Flemish towns: the manufacturing interests were much too jealous and too strong to allow Englishmen to invade the local monopoly; and accordingly the Merchant Adventurers were compelled to turn elsewhere. In 1407 they established themselves for the first time at Antwerp, by the favour of the Duke of Brabant. Antwerp was then quite a small town, insignificant in comparison with Bruges; and the Duke, who wanted to benefit by the duties the English importers would pay him, could afford to disregard the remonstrances of the few weavers and cloth merchants there might happen to be in

Economic Organisation

his capital. For a good many years the Adventurers were not quite satisfied with Antwerp as their centre, and made various attempts to get a footing in some busier place; but after 1444 they settled down at Antwerp for good, and remained there till the town was ruined by the religious troubles of the next century and the disastrous siege of 1584. Their presence certainly contributed to the astounding growth of Antwerp in wealth and population and trade, a growth which by the middle of the sixteenth century placed it in a position in relation to western European markets as strong as that which Bruges had occupied in previous centuries. But although the English Adventurers might seem to be as definitely localised as the Staplers, and there might appear to be little difference in their methods of business, they really breathed a more independent and enterprising air. They were not bound by governmental regulations to the same extent as the Staplers; the cloth export was an expanding business, while the woollen trade was a stationary or declining one; and when the great era of geographical discovery began at the end of the fifteenth century, it was the Merchant Adventurers who were most eager and able to push out into new directions. Out of their circle arose all the Tudor companies for adventuring into distant parts for purposes of trade —the Russia Company, the Levant Company, and, greatest of all, the East India Company; so that they may be regarded in a very real sense as the founders of English foreign trade.

The appearance and progress of the Merchant

Capital and Investment

Adventurers indicate the advent on a considerable scale of a new factor in English economic development, the factor of Capital (as distinguished from Land and Labour); and the advent also of the phenomenon, historically inextricable from Capital, which we call Investment. By Capital the business world has always meant—whatever the economists may have tried to mean—wealth which its owner can employ for the purpose of gain; and by Investment we meant partly the external, or business, fact that there really exist openings for the use of wealth in directions which will bring an income or "revenue," over and above the return of the sum employed; and partly the internal, or psychological, fact that its owners are actually desirous of using it in such directions. And the early history of the Merchant Adventurers shows us how this trading capital came into existence in England. It did not arise out of the revenues of the great landlords, as some have conjectured; the younger sons of the lesser gentry might go into business but they certainly carried no capital with them. More was probably made at first out of the profits of tax-collecting; and it is possible that some of the townsmen who earliest engaged in trade were enriched by their ownership of land made valuable by the growth of an urban population. But the chief source, it would appear, of the capital now turning in the direction of foreign enterprise was the wealth already acquired by merchants, whether of native or foreign extraction, in the home trade, and especially in the importation into England and the sale there of foreign commodities in demand among the upper and middle classes.

Economic Organisation

In dealing in an earlier lecture with the craft gilds I probably gave the impression that they were all composed of comparatively humble handicraftsmen; and this was perhaps unavoidable. But early in the fourteenth century we notice that out of the multitude of crafts or misteries a few companies had already become conspicuous for the wealth and influence of their members, both in London and in the other chief trading centres of the realm. In London—where before the end of the reign of Edward III there were as many as 48 "misteries" sufficiently organised to send representatives to the Common Council—some twelve "great companies" are soon conspicuous above the rest—viz. the Mercers, Grocers, Drapers, Fishmongers, Goldsmiths, Skinners, Merchant Tailors, Haberdashers, Salters, Ironmongers, Vintners, and Clothmakers. Now all these trades required a certain amount of capital. The Goldsmiths, for instance, used an expensive raw material; and though the master goldsmith continued to work with his own hands at the more delicate operations—as we may see him represented in engravings of a somewhat later period—the prosperous men of the craft naturally occupied a superior social position. Much the same is true of the Tailors, at a time when the upper classes dressed so expensively. The Fishmongers needed capital for their fishing smacks; and so on. And the three companies which were early placed at the head of the list, the Mercers, Grocers, and Drapers, and which make their appearance in each of the larger towns as well as in London, were all composed of men who were exclusively traders and not manufacturers at

Capital and Investment

all. The Drapers arose perhaps out of the Shearmen, who actually prepared the cloth for use ; but they soon left the work of shearing to others, and confined themselves to purchase and sale : the importance of their company testifies to the rapid extension of the manufacture of cloth in England. The Grocers, on the other hand, were quite clearly from the first either importers, or else dealers in imported commodities. Their wares were all kinds of spices and drugs, and their very name (*Grossiers*) implies that their operations were wholesale. The Mercers, likewise, who traded in "merceries"—linen, canvas, and above all silk fabrics —derived their name from the fact that they were dealers and handled "wares" (*mercimonia*). From several of these companies the Merchant Adventurers were recruited : each Adventurer continued to belong to his own city company—and indeed they were bound to belong to one of the misteries if they wished to enjoy the municipal franchise—while engaging in the new foreign enterprise. But it was with the Mercers that they were most closely associated. And how much capital a successful Mercer might accumulate we can gather from the story of Whittington, "thrice Lord Mayor of London," in 1398, 1407, and 1420.

There had, it is true, been wealthy merchants and financiers in London long before, and they had formed a conspicuous element in the civic oligarchy. They were, however, largely of foreign origin ; some were Gascon, like the Mayor of Bordeaux in 1275 who became Mayor of London in 1280 ; others were Italian, like the leading men among the Pepperers, the forerunners of the Grocers. Merchants of English

Economic Organisation

descent were only beginning to make their way into considerable operations, and they were commonly connected in business with aliens controlling a larger capital who could supply them with imported goods on credit. But by the middle of the fourteenth century the situation had changed. English-owned capital now made foreign capital unnecessary for the home trade; and Englishmen had sufficiently large resources, as well as sufficient courage and sufficient knowledge how to deal with foreign tariffs and foreign currency, to venture upon overseas trade on their own account.

It is often said that the teaching of the mediæval Church with regard to Usury, enforced as it was by secular legislation and by the law courts, failed to recognise "the productive character of capital," and put obstacles in the way of the progress of trade. Such assertions show ignorance of the historical development. During the later Middle Ages, what we know as "capital" was only beginning to come into existence : the world, that is to say, was only beginning to see accumulations of wealth which could be invested in any direction in trade and industry, and to realise that opportunities for such investment actually existed. Now any investment in which the owner of capital actually "adventured" his property and took a real risk, in the hope of obtaining some return over and above the sum he put in, was regarded by theologians and the ecclesiastical (or "canonist") lawyers as perfectly legitimate. So that, instead of retarding the free growth of trade, the Church may be even said to have stimulated it, by employing its influence to turn the

Capital and Investment

disposable wealth of the time away from mere loans to impecunious rulers or extravagant grandees or mismanaging monasteries—loans which might fairly be described in most instances by the modern term "unproductive" or the mediæval term "barren"—into the more productive paths of commercial venture. This point of view is clearly expressed in the speech with which Morton, the Cardinal Archbishop of Canterbury, who was also Lord Chancellor of England, addressed one of the early parliaments of Henry VII. "His Grace (the King) prays you," he says, "to take into consideration matters of trade, as also the manufactures of the kingdom, and to restrain the bastard and barren employment of moneys to usury and unlawful exchanges; that they may be, as their natural use is, turned upon commerce and lawful and royal trading."

In the south of Europe the capitalist organisation which sprang up to meet the new needs of trade was the *Societas*, the partnership or company (we may call it either) trading on a joint-stock; either in its simple form, where all the partners alike took part in the management, or in the special form adapted to the needs of sea-going enterprise, known as the *commenda*, and reappearing in England in these recent years in what is known as "limited partnership." But in England the habit of forming gilds was too all-pervasive, and satisfied for a long time too completely all the needs of the situation, to allow the joint-stock plan to appear until much later, and then not as the accompaniment of a *societas* on south-European lines, but as the inevitable but tardy creation of the gild or fellowship itself, trading

Economic Organisation

in distant regions. No doubt there were occasionally, even in England, family partnerships; and there were also occasionally quite large partnerships formed for various enterprises within the country, such as the development of mines. But there is no trace of any such large partnerships among Englishmen engaged in foreign trade; and indeed the rules of the fellowship of Merchant Adventurers, which, like all other industrial and commercial gilds, insisted upon a regular apprenticeship for each of its members, might easily stand in the way. So long as a fellowship of traders (or "company" in the English sense) was able to come to terms with foreign princes, and from the common subscriptions, or possibly from contributions in proportion to the individual trade done, was able to provide the necessary establishment or "house" in the staple town, it sufficed that the Adventurers should trade on their individual stocks. But when in 1553 a number of "adventurers" created "the mystery and company of the Merchant Adventurers for the discovery of regions, dominions, islands, and places unknown" at a great distance—to wit, in Russia—and their agents had to reach that country by way of the White Sea, and then penetrate for hundreds of miles inland to the capital, it was evident that individual trading was out of the question. The year 1553, therefore, saw the formation of the first true joint-stock company: and it is interesting to notice that the number of members or shareholders was 240, and the shares £25 each. The example thus set was imitated by several others of the companies engaged in business overseas, and above all, half a century later, by the East India Company But the

Capital and Investment

transition to the new corporate plan was not complete even yet. For the joint-stock in the case of the Russia Company, as afterwards in that of the East India Company, was limited to each separate voyage, and the profits were divided after each voyage in proportion to the investment. It took some time to learn by troublesome experience that the business of each voyage could not be kept completely apart and separately accounted for ; and that a permanent joint-stock, not periodically repaid, was the only convenient arrangement.

We are, however, rather outstripping the point we have reached in the narrative. The great expansion of England's foreign trade in the fifteenth century, and the first half of the sixteenth, was the work of the Merchant Adventurers, and they never reached the point of having a common stock. As time went on, the tutelage in which the merchants of the Hanse and of Italy sought to hold the trade of this country became more and more irksome. The English Adventurers sought to enter into the geographical spheres of monopoly or influence which the Hansards and the Venetians kept jealously for themselves. Demands for reciprocity fell on deaf ears ; and the inevitable outcome was only delayed by the fact that the English monarchs hesitated to give up the revenue they derived from the foreigners, and to endanger the political friendship of the powers they represented. First the Venetians lost their privileged position in 1534 : they had obstinately refused to let the English merchants enter the Levant to share their trade in Malmsey wine and currants. Within half a century, with the favour of the

Economic Organisation

Sultan, who was ready enough to favour the rivals of his ancient enemies, the Venetians, the Levant Company was regularly established in the eastern Mediterranean, and supplying England with the commodities for which it had been previously dependent on Venice. With the Hanse the bickering went on much longer. While the Venetians were being driven to give up their annual visits, the German merchants in the Steelyard still maintained their proud position. When Holbein came to England he found employment in painting the leading members of the community; and the pageant he designed for them on the occasion of the coronation procession of Anne Boleyn cast into the shade all the like productions of the city companies. Their complete satisfaction with themselves is illustrated by the allegorical picture they commissioned Holbein to produce for their hall: side by side with the mediæval conception of "The Triumph of Poverty" it displayed the modern and commercial conception of "The Triumph of Wealth," with all her appropriate train of virtues. It was not till 1597 that the German merchants, refusing definitely to let English traders into their German preserves, finally lost their privileges and left the Steelyard. But by that time the old unity of the Hanse was already breaking up. What the Adventurers could not obtain from the Hanse as a whole, they were able to obtain from one of the constituent towns. The year 1611 saw them, after many vicissitudes, finally established in Hamburg and in the possession of lucrative privileges. From this time dates the close connection between Hamburg and England, which was so important a branch of the

Capital and Investment

trading relations of this country during the seventeenth and the early part of the eighteenth century. From Hamburg the Merchant Adventurers were able to find a market for their cloth over the whole of northern Germany; and there the "English Court" remained, until it was broken up by the orders of Napoleon in 1806.

LECTURE V

Domestic Industry and Tudor Nationalism

WE have already seen the fundamental importance of the woollen industry for English economic development. It furnishes the explanation of the far-reaching agricultural changes of the fifteenth and sixteenth centuries : it provided the commodity with which England first entered actively into the world's commerce. Its significance can hardly be overestimated. It was the first of the great manufactures of England ; it created a basis for English activity and wealth before iron and cotton ; and in the seventeenth and early eighteenth centuries it accounted for more than two-thirds of our exports. Its power is shown by the remarkable fact that it was able to bring about a complete reversal of the trade policy of the country. The export of English wool, which had once been the pivot of the government's finance and the chief occasion for commercial intercourse with foreign countries, was from 1660 to 1825 absolutely prohibited. It remains now to look at the internal organisation of the industry; and here again we shall find that it presented phenomena of the utmost interest. In the centuries before improvements in transportation made it possible for Europe to provide itself with the cotton of Asia or America, at a time

Domestic Industry

when the use of furs and silks was necessarily confined to the wealthier classes, woollen fabrics were the common, over large areas practically the only, wear of the great mass of the people. The organisation of their production had accordingly a typical significance: it exemplified, in all countries and in well-nigh every district, and in a clear and unmistakable form, the shapes which industrial relations were bound to take under the varying conditions of the time. As soon as specialised industrial workers made their appearance, occupied mainly in manufacture and grouped together for the most part in the towns, the shape was what we now know as the gild system, and of this we have already noticed the leading characteristics. There is much that is still obscure in the municipal history of the twelfth and thirteenth centuries; but it is surely not uninstructive that in all the large towns of western Europe gilds of woollen weavers should have arisen and made themselves conspicuous during that period, and that only second to them in prominence should have been gilds of fullers and dyers engaged in other and later processes in cloth manufacture. The appearance of such societies, a century or more before many other craftsmen began to draw together in fellowship, can only be explained by their greater number—itself due to the more primary character of the want which their products satisfied.

But as the woollen industry was the first, on any considerable scale, to take the gild form, it was the first to break away from it; and this for the same reason—the extent of the demand. England was capable of producing large supplies of wool, of good quality.

Economic Organisation

What was first lacking was technical skill. Whatever may be the case to-day, the economic history of earlier centuries fully bears out the contention of Frederick List that the creation of "productive powers" is more important for a nation than the mere possession of "values in exchange." And England owes its productive powers very largely to the alien immigrants who have made their way to her, with or without welcome. The necessary skill in handicraft in the woollen industry came to the country from the Netherlands chiefly during two periods. There was a considerable migration from the Low Countries during the reign of Edward III, and again some two centuries later, during the early years of Elizabeth. In the one case they were driven from home by internal dissensions—by the contest between the great weaving cities of Ghent and Ypres and their count, and by the collision of interest between the large towns and the surrounding country districts. In the second case they were driven away by the religious persecutions of Alva. It is with the first of these migrations that we have now to do; for the change in the organisation of industry made itself clearly manifest long before the time of Elizabeth.

A rough and rude cloth was apparently produced at one time in every town in the country. The weaver would usually come into direct contact with his customer or employer : I add "employer," because undoubtedly it was often the practice for the weaver to work up an employer's yarn. But with the improvement here and there in the weaver's art, the manufacture, at any rate of the better qualities, would tend to concentrate itself in particular localities. Sheep,

Domestic Industry

again, were raised all over the country; and we have seen that in the fifteenth and sixteenth centuries the inducement to grow wool was strong enough to bring about enclosures in most of the Midland counties. In time the natural advantages of the downs and moors and of counties like Leicester and Lincoln would make them the homes of the larger flocks; and accordingly wool merchants (or "wool staplers") became even more necessary than before to collect the raw material and convey it to users elsewhere in England or abroad, or to foreign merchants in London and other ports. Nor was this all: as early as the fourteenth century we can trace the rise of a body of dealers in cloth, numerous enough in the country generally to need a market provided for them in London at Blackwell Hall in 1397, and rich enough in London and the other great towns to take rank among the wealthiest of the city companies. Doubtless these dealers, or "drapers" as they were called, were engaged not only in collecting cloth for sale in parts of England at a distance from the place of production, but also in collecting it for export abroad. What their presence indicates is the growing distance between the producer and the consumer, and the need for commercial middlemen.

But as the market widened, the opportunity for middlemen and their services to production would become even greater. Such a widening of the market came with the growth and extension of the foreign market for cloth, and we can ascribe this roughly to the second half of the fifteenth century.

If we can regard the number of pieces on which the

Economic Organisation

Hansards paid duty as an index of the whole trade of the country, we may conclude that the export of cloth, which grew comparatively slowly—perhaps by fifty per cent.—during the first half of the fifteenth century, actually trebled itself during the second half. And during that period we find four vital changes in industrial organisation taking place. First, the weaving of cloth and the allied branches of the manufacture are leaving the towns and establishing themselves in villages and hamlets and isolated cottages over the countryside; secondly, with the abandonment by the workpeople of the towns, the gild association also drops asunder in the woollen industry, though the State still, as we shall see, enforces the rule of apprenticeship; thirdly, the industry concentrates itself in certain particular districts — "the shires which use cloth-making," as a contemporary historian calls them—those shires being chiefly Norfolk, Suffolk, and Essex in the east, Wilts, Somerset, and Devon in the west; and finally, a new class of *entrepreneurs* appear—the "clothiers," as they are called, who now control the whole process of production. Their essential function, as the great Elizabethan Statute of Apprentices phrases it, was to "put cloth to making." An Act of 1465 reveals conditions precisely similar to those which were found still in existence more than three hundred and forty years later by the famous parliamentary Committee of 1806: the clothier "delivering the wool" to be carded and spun, then giving out the yarn to the weaver to be woven into cloth, and then placing the cloth in the hands of the fuller, "walker," or "tucker" to be felted and cleansed.

Domestic Industry

This remarkable transformation raises more questions than we are at present able to solve. Where, we may ask, did the capital and enterprise come from, which are indicated by the advent of the clothiers? Probably from many directions, but especially from among the ranks of the drapers or cloth-dealers: it was natural that men engaged in selling cloth should undertake to procure its manufacture by themselves purchasing the wool and getting the yarn spun, and providing poor weavers with the necessary materials. Where did the country weavers come from? Probably from the less successful craftsmen and, especially, from among the discontented journeymen of the towns, now becoming a separate industrial class, and unable to look forward to finding places for themselves in the narrow circle of "masters." However it may have been brought about, we have reached, it will be seen, the third of the stages we have already distinguished in the evolution of industry—the stage marked by the dominance of a commercial middleman who finds material and employment for the artisan. Economists are accustomed, we have already noticed, to call this condition of things by the not very satisfactory terms, "domestic system," or *Haus-industrie*, from the fact that—in contrast with "the factory system" that followed—the process of manufacture still took place at the workman's own home. Whatever we call it, there is evidently to be discerned here an intermediate or a transition stage between the gild system with its independent handicraftsmen and the factory with its mass of congregated workpeople. Capital first accumulated in trade now turned back,

Economic Organisation

so to speak, on industry, and began to take the control of the manufacturing operations. And the appearance of the same system in the textile industries of other countries—as, for instance, the linen manufacture of Holland and Silesia and the silk manufacture of France—and indeed in all considerable manufactures that sprang up before the advent of machinery, such as Sheffield cutlery in the seventeenth century and the English hat and boot trades in the eighteenth, seems to indicate that it was the natural consequence of the economic forces at work. When goods were made by small masters in little workshops, the only way in which manufacture could be quickly stimulated to meet a rapidly growing demand was for capitalists to come forward, provide the materials, and undertake the business of finding a market.

The economic situation in England, as elsewhere, was complicated by the fact that, while the large new industry grew up with its new organisation in the villages of certain districts, many of the old trades, supplying only local or limited demands, continued for a long time to be carried on in the towns by independent master artisans, associated in companies which were the direct representatives and descendants of the mediæval gilds. They continued to exist, but they are no longer typical of the wider occupations of the country. And it is significant that when in 1712 a pamphleteer drew the character of an Englishman under the name that has since stuck to him of "John Bull," he depicted him as a clothier, whose ordinary talk was of "the affairs of Blackwell Hall, and the price of broadcloth, wool, and bays."

Tudor Nationalism

It is, however, now time to introduce a factor which can hardly escape the notice of any careful student of the Tudor period: and that is the part played by the regulating power of the national State. England, from the time of the establishment of the strong rule of her Norman kings, had never so completely escaped from the control of a central government as some of the continental countries. The legal and administrative machinery elaborated by Henry II and his successors, the legislative activity of Parliament under the third Edward, these had brought the whole country in large measure within the scope of a single all-embracing political system. Over large parts of the Continent, in the later Middle Ages, central national authority was non-existent or exceedingly weak; and its place in the regulation of economic life was taken by the authorities of the various towns and cities. The unit of industrial and commercial relations was the town, and neither the nation nor, as later in Germany, the "territory" or principality. England, in this as in other economic respects—such as the prevalence of the manorial system and the appearance of the gild—was not unlike the rest of western Europe. In England also we may characterise the period of the later Middle Ages as a period of "town-economy." Yet the several municipalities were never quite so free from external control as in Italy or Germany; and we have already seen examples of the far-reaching influence of the central government in certain directions, *e.g.* in the regulation of the staple.

But when we come to the age of the Tudors the hold of the central government over the economic life

Economic Organisation

of the people becomes far more clear and unmistakable. This was the natural outcome in the economic sphere of the wonderful outburst of the spirit of nationality which characterises the latter part of the epoch. The nation felt itself to be one, as never before; having this feeling of unity it was natural that it should wish to see its ideals carried out over the whole country; and to do this it turned to the government as representative of the national will.

The machinery of Tudor rule was threefold. First there was the Parliament to give legislative force to national policy. The period is marked by a series of great statutes vitally affecting the organisation of economic life : the two most outstanding examples being what was called in later ages the Statute of Apprentices, soon after Elizabeth came to the throne (1563), and the great Poor Law, almost at the end of her reign (1601), which brought to a definite conclusion a series of experiments in the way of legislation stretching over more than sixty years. We cannot, indeed, attribute to Parliament during this period any really independent initiative apart from the monarch and his advisers. Parliament existed to give information about the needs of the country, and to give the support of national agreement and acquiescence to the measures already decided upon by the wisdom of the government. It was only its usefulness for this purpose which enabled it to survive during the absolutism of Henry VIII. For the greater part of the period, the real pivot, on which everything turned, was that second part of the mechanism of government —the Council. The Council both dictated legislation and enforced it when it had been passed. It is very

Tudor Nationalism

significant that while the prayer for the High Court of Parliament was not composed till the stormy times of Charles I's first parliament, and was not made a regular part of the English Church service till 1662, the Book of Common Prayer contained, from its earliest form as drawn up in 1549, two prayers for the Council—one in the Litany and one in the Communion office. This sufficiently illustrates the place which it occupied in the public eye. And the third great element in the Tudor system was the local executive machinery—that of the Justices of the Peace, acting individually, or in association with their fellows in Quarter Sessions. The office of Justice of the Peace had been growing up ever since the reign of Edward III, and with it had been incorporated the office of Justice of Labourers which had been created to carry out the labour legislation called forth by the Black Death. But it was not till the Tudor period that it reached its definitive form.

The place which the Justices of the Peace took henceforward in the political and social system of England is altogether unique; and of this English public men were fully aware. "It is such a form of subordinate government for the tranquillity and quiet of the realm," wrote the great Chief Justice, Sir Edward Coke, "as no part of the Christian world hath the like." Elsewhere national governments, in the machinery at their disposal for the administration of the provinces, were limited to one of two alternatives. Either local administration had to be left to local magnates—these in the country districts, of course, being the larger landlords—and this meant the survival of feudalism.

Economic Organisation

Or the central government planted in the several districts a number of professional officials, who were sent down from the capital and who, if they had no local partialities and interests, had also no local affections or influence: and thus was constituted a bureaucracy. England alone—for good or for ill, we must not hastily say which—was able in large measure to combine the virtues of both methods. The Justices were, in fact, the local squires, with all their local knowledge and weight; but they derived their authority from a royal commission, and they carried on their work under the inspection and control of the Council at the centre of government.

The drawback to the system—and every system has its drawbacks — was that the agency through which the government was compelled to act was an agency with an inevitable class bias. Yet it was not till, in the latter half of the seventeenth century, the effective supervision and, if need were, coercion by the Council were withdrawn, that the defects of English adminstrative machinery began to outweigh its merits.

Let us now look at the policy pursued by the Council, confirmed by Parliament and enforced through the Justices; or rather at the principles at the back of it. These principles were those of the great thinkers of the Middle Ages, now applied to the whole country and enforced by a national authority. They started from the idea not of liberty but of order. A State should be well ordered; and by well ordered was understood a grouping of its subjects in due ranks, each with its proper duties and responsibilities.

Tudor Nationalism

"The heavens themselves,"

Shakespeare, in the last months of Elizabeth's reign, makes one of his characters say, in *Troilus and Cressida*,

> "the planets and this centre
> Observe degree, priority and place,
> Insisture, course, proportion, season, form,
> Office and custom, in all line of order."

And he goes on to express the current view of the thoughtful men of the time that even "enterprise"—by which he means the proper activity of citizens in their several positions—was dependent on the maintenance of "degree."

> "O, when degree is shaked,
> Which is the ladder to all high designs,
> Then enterprise is sick! How could communities,
> Degrees in schools and brotherhoods in cities,
> Peaceful commerce from dividable shores,
> The premogeniture and due of birth,
> Prerogative of age, crowns, sceptres, laurels,
> But by degree, stand in authentic place?
> Take but degree away, untune that string,
> And hark, what discord follows."

And so in the Catechism, set forth in 1549 to be learnt by every child, high or low, before he was brought to be confirmed by the bishop, the compendium of duty ended with the statement that it behoved everyone "to learn and labour truly to get mine own living, and to do my duty in that state of life unto which it shall please God to call me"—not, be it observed, " hath pleased God," as shown merely in the fact of birth. The men of Tudor times supposed, no doubt, that for most people their "state of life" was practically settled

Economic Organisation

by their birth; but they never believed in rigid castes, and they always recognised that a man might be called by God to a state of life other than that in which he was born. But in whatever state or degree he found himself, of that degree he was to do the duty.

But to do it he would need training. And that training it was believed to be the duty of the government to see that he got. Hence the great Statute of Apprentices of 5 Elizabeth, cap. 4, which extended to the whole nation and to all manufacturing industries the seven years' obligatory apprenticeship which had hitherto been enforced by the several misteries backed up by the municipalities. "It shall not be lawful to any person, other than such as do now lawfully exercise any occupation, to exercise any craft now used within the realm of England and Wales, except he shall have been brought up therein seven years at the least as apprentice . . . nor to set any person on work in such occupation, being not a workman at this day, except he shall have been apprentice." The use of the word "now"—"now used within the realm"—was certainly not intended as a limitation: but the judges in the eighteenth century ruled that the effect of it was to limit the statute to industries already established in 1563; so that (and this is an important fact) the new cotton trade and the new iron trade which came into existence in the eighteenth century were never subject to any statutory prescription as to apprenticeship, however common—in the cotton trade in particular—the practice may in fact have become in imitation of the usage in other trades.

Tudor Nationalism

Having been properly trained, every man, it was assumed, could find suitable employment. How it was proposed to deal with cases where that assumption was falsified by events, we shall learn in a moment. Finding employment, it was generally held that men should receive a suitable wage ; and to this conviction the government sought to give effect by the system of Justices' Assessments, under the control of the Council. Ever since the Black Death, Parliament had attempted to determine the rates of remuneration for agricultural labour. We must be careful not to interpret this policy as the outcome merely of selfishness on the part of the landlords. The public opinion of all educated men was on the side of the public authorities in applying to labour the general principle of "just price." It seemed as evidently immoral to ask for higher wages because the ranks of labour were thinned by pestilence, as (to take an instance which actually occurred) to try to get a higher price for tiles because the town was unroofed by a tempest. To leave such things to the operation of the Supply and Demand of the moment was to abandon the duty and task of government. The attitude in this matter of William Langland, who wrote his *Vision of Piers the Plowman* about 1377, is highly significant. It is usual to contrast Langland with Chaucer, the man of the people with the man of the court. J. R. Green, for instance, describes him as "the gaunt poet of the poor." And yet Langland has no sympathy with

"labourers landless, that live by their hands,"

and, not content with "worts a day old," "penny ale,"

Economic Organisation

and "a piece of good bacon," clamour for "fresh flesh or fish":

> "He must highly be hired, or else will he chide,
> Bewailing his woe as a workman to live . . .
> He curses the King and his Council after,
> Who license the laws that the labourers grieve."

Langland warns them harshly that a time of dearth will soon come and reduce them to a more patient frame of mind.

The difficulties, which were always considerable, in enforcing the statutes of labourers were increased in the middle of the sixteenth century by the rise in prices, due first to the debasement of the currency during the government of Henry VIII and Edward VI, and then by the influx of silver from the newly discovered mines of America. Yet these difficulties were far from inducing the government to leave wages to free contract: their effect was only to lead the government to substitute scales of wages varying with the cost of living for the rigidly fixed rates of earlier statutes. The great statute of 1563 (5 Eliz., cap. 4), already referred to, began by confessing that the existing laws with regard to wages could not "conveniently"—"respecting the advancement of prices "—"be put in due execution without the greatest grief and burden of the poor labourer and hired man." What was therefore necessary, it went on to say, was legislation which would "yield unto the hired person, both in the time of scarcity and in the time of plenty, a convenient proportion of wages." Accordingly it enacted that the Justices of the Peace of every shire or town, at every Easter Sessions, "calling unto them such discreet and grave persons . . . as

Tudor Nationalism

they shall think meet, and conferring together respecting the plenty or scarcity of the time," should " have authority to rate and appoint the wages " of all labourers, artificers, &c. These rates they were to certify to Chancery; "whereupon it shall be lawful for the Lord Chancellor, upon declaration thereof to the Queen . . . or to the Lords or others of the Privy Council . . . to cause to be printed and sent down proclamations concerning the several rates appointed." " If " in any year "it shall happen that there be no need of any alteration, then the proclamation for the year past shall remain in force."

It was "pollitiquely intended" — *i.e.* consciously aimed at as a matter of State policy—as a later statute puts it, that the regulation of wages should extend to all manual occupations. But doubts were raised as to whether the statute was intended to cover persons employed in " domestic " industry, like the weavers working for clothiers; first, because the original act seemed to lay stress only on workers in husbandry and on the particular crafts which had previously been regulated, and, secondly, because it had implied that the wages were to be time wages, while in the woollen industry, in the form it had now assumed, payment was generally made by the piece. Accordingly, by a statute of 1597–8 (39 Eliz., cap. 12), the authority of the Justices was expressly defined to include the rating of wages "of any labourers, weavers, spinsters and workmen or workwomen whatsoever, either working by day, week, month or year, or taking any work, at any person's hand whatsoever, to be done," *i.e.* as piecework. That there was felt to be some need to inter-

Economic Organisation

vene for the protection of the domestic weavers is shown by the fact that an act of 1603-4 (1 Jac., cap. 6) not only confirmed this definition of the Justices' authority, but went on to enact that "if any clothier or other shall refuse to obey the said assessment of wages, and shall not pay so much or so great wages to their weavers, spinsters, workmen or workwomen as shall be appointed ... that then every clothier and other person so offending shall forfeit for every such offence, to the party grieved, ten shillings." As an afterthought it occurred to the legislators that many of the clothiers had prospered so far as to be made Justices themselves, and that these clothier Justices might have too much influence in Quarter Sessions. A separate section was accordingly tacked on to the act with this significant proviso, "that no clothier being a justice of peace ... shall be any rater of any wages for any weaver, tucker, spinster or other artisan that dependeth upon the making of cloth."

The clear implication of a clause like this helps us, I think, to arrive at a conclusion as to the character of the legislation as a whole. It has been represented by some writers as a huge conspiracy of the employing classes to keep down wages. I cannot agree with them. I think it was an honest attempt to secure for every employed person what should be a fitting wage, and a wage that should vary with the cost of living; although it is quite obvious that in deciding what was "a convenient proportion of wages," *i.e.* wages suitable to the position of "the hired person," the Justices of the Peace would not be likely to err on the side of extravagance. And the

Tudor Nationalism

case of the clothier Justices shows that the government were fully aware of the possibility of selfish bias, and would do what they could to counteract it. It is another question how far the act was obeyed by the Justices, and still another how far the assessments were observed. When the subject began to be discussed, some thirty years ago, only about a dozen assessments of various dates between 1593 and 1684 were known to exist. But since then more than a hundred others have come to light; sufficient to prove that, throughout the seventeenth century, the annual assessment was part of the ordinary business of every Easter Sessions. There is much also to suggest that on the whole the assessments were conformed to by employers. But how far or how long the assessments kept pace with the cost of living we have as yet hardly enough evidence to decide. The comparisons sometimes instituted between the movement of assessed wages and the movement of the price of wheat are not quite conclusive; because the Justices would properly take into account the whole range of a labourer's wants and not the single article of wheaten bread. As the Essex Justices declared in 1651, it was their duty to have "special regard and consideration to the prices at this time of all kinds of victuals and apparel, both linen and woollen, and *all* the necessary charges." It is only in the last year or so that statisticians have succeeded in constructing "index numbers" to show the variation in the cost of living of working-people in the twentieth century: for the seventeenth and eighteenth centuries the index numbers have still to be calculated.

Economic Organisation

In the first half of the eighteenth century, the practice of assessment gradually fell into disuse. So completely was it disregarded in the cloth industry that in 1756, on the petition of the woollen weavers of Gloucester, an act was passed giving the Justices authority to fix wages by the ell, regardless of the fact that they already had that power by the unrepealed statute of Elizabeth. In 1757, on the petition of the clothiers, the act was repealed, and with it, by implication, the wage assessment clauses of the act of 1563, so far as the woollen trade was concerned, since it was now enacted that wages should in future be settled by free contract between the parties. The reason assigned was that a prescribed weaving wage per ell, or unit of length, was incompatible with the great variety in the width of various kinds of cloth and in the weight of the yarn employed. The abandonment in 1757 of State regulation of wages in what was then the one really great industry of England is very significant. It shows that the system of regulating wages was abandoned long before the advent of machinery or the factory. It was thrown off by employers in an industry still in the domestic stage and still making no use of "power." And the excuse given was not without a certain force. With the multiplication of varieties of product, a wage list to be appropriate must become proportionately detailed and elaborate. This is what is being discovered to-day in all attempts to settle rates of wages either by joint agreement or by statutory boards. It is likely enough that the Justices in the eighteenth century had not the necessary technical knowledge.

Tudor Nationalism

In the years which followed 1757, the only serious attempt to regulate wages by the authority of the Justices is to be found in the so-called Spitalfields Acts which were passed in 1773 for the benefit of the London silk-weavers, and were tolerably successful, though restricted in their operation to London and not affecting the cheaper silk manufactures of Coventry and Macclesfield. The legislation was effective, partly because the article produced was of the nature of a luxury, partly because the Justices allowed themselves, in the rates they fixed, to be guided by agreements between employers and employed. So successful on the whole was the arrangement in this particular case that the Spitalfields Acts were suffered to remain unrepealed till 1824, in spite of the fact that the act of Elizabeth for the regulation of wages generally had been repealed in 1813. The powers of the Justices in respect of wages certainly left no bitter memories behind them. For in the distress of the Industrial Revolution it again and again occurred to various bodies of workpeople to appeal to the act of 5 Elizabeth and petition that it should again be enforced. The reply of Parliament to these embarrassing requests was to abrogate the act altogether.

Not quite a century afterwards, legislation began to retrace its steps. By the act of 1909, Trade Boards were established by the State to "fix minimum rates of wages" in certain trades popularly spoken of as "sweated": in the language of the act, trades in which "the rate of wages is exceptionally low." The Boards are composed not only of an equal number of representatives of employers and workers, but also of such

Economic Organisation

a number of "appointed members" as the Board of Trade may think fit, short of half that of the representative members, and they are presided over by an "appointed" chairman. The numbers of the "appointed" members in the first five Boards have been 3 out of a total of 15, 3 out of 35, 3 out of 19, 5 out of 21, and 3 out of 11 respectively. They are all persons of approved tact, and doubtless they seek by patient diplomacy to obtain the largest possible measure of agreement: but it is perfectly clear that they hold the balance of power. In 1912 a much longer step was taken, and statutory machinery set up to "settle" "minimum rates of wages," together with the necessary "district rules," for all the underground workers in the coal mines of the country. That machinery consists in the last resort of the individual chairmen of the several Joint District Boards, inasmuch as they are directed themselves to settle the rates and rules, if any Board fails to reach an agreement; and these chairmen are appointed, in default of agreement, by the Board of Trade. Wages under these acts are just as much "regulated by the State" as ever were those fixed by the Justices' assessments. They are State-regulated in two senses: in the sense that they are not determined by free contract between the parties concerned (either individuals or associations), but by an authority which derives its power from the State; and in the sense that this authority in the last resort lies in the hands of persons nominated by the executive of the State. To control wages through local bodies with statutory powers, even if they are in some degree representative, is as much State control as to do so directly from

Tudor Nationalism

Whitehall. The more immediately practical problem to-day is not whether free contract shall be superseded by State control, but what are the wisest methods of exercising State control. I may add that before we criticise the vague language—"a convenient proportion of wages"—of the act of Elizabeth, we may ask ourselves whether the legislation of Edward VII and George V is even equally explicit as to the principles on which the determination shall rest. In directing the authorities to get information about "the plenty or scarcity of the time," the legislation of 1563 at any rate recognised that consideration as to cost of living which the legislation of 1909–12 passed by in silence.

To return, however, to other features of the Tudor policy. Having been properly trained and being secured in a "convenient" wage, it was everyone's duty to work; and it was assumed by statute after statute that employment could be found by everyone who cared to take it. The vagrancy of sturdy beggars was sternly prohibited, in a series of statutes of ever-growing severity. Such persons were to be openly whipped (said a statute of 1598) "until his or her body be bloody, and forthwith sent from parish to parish the straight way to the parish where he was born if the same way be known, and if not, to the parish where he last dwelt one whole year, there to put himself to labour as a true subject ought to do." If he had no parish "settlement," as it was called, he was to be conveyed to the house of correction (whose establishment the act authorised), "there to remain and be employed in work until he shall be placed in some service."

Economic Organisation

But all the destitute were not "sturdy," *i.e.* able to earn their living if they chose. It was gradually borne in upon the minds of the men of the sixteenth century, that, besides "idle and loitering persons and valiant beggars," there were "impotent, feeble and lame, which are the poor in very deed." These must be assisted; no worthy person should be allowed to starve in a well-ordered State; and accordingly for the relief of the "poor in very deed," the Tudor government gradually built up the Poor Law, which reached its definite form in the statute of 1601. The real starting point was the act of 1536, which imposed on the several parishes the duty of relieving their own destitute poor. Notice in passing that this was one, and the most important, of those statutes which made the ecclesiastical division of the country, the parish, *i.e.* the area attached to the village church, the unit of administration for civil purposes. The authority of the local Justice and the machinery of the parish now began to take the place in the life of the people which the lord of the manor and the manorial court had previously occupied: and this was the easier because in rural districts the parish and the Justice in a large proportion of cases were only the manor and its lord under other names. And the explanation of the use made of the ecclesiastical parish is largely to be found in the history of the Poor Law. The Poor Law grew out of a plan to regulate voluntary charity. At first it was thought to be enough that the churchwardens of every parish should take "discreet and convenient order, by gathering and procuring of charitable and voluntary alms of the good christian people within the same with boxes

Tudor Nationalism

every sunday, holyday, and other festival day and otherwise," and that the parsons "in all and every their sermons . . . as in time of all confessions and at the making of wills should exhort, move, stir and provoke people to be liberal"; and it was expressly laid down that, when voluntary alms would not suffice, the parishioners were not to be "constrained to any such certain contribution but as their free wills and charities shall extend." But organised charity broke down then, as it has so frequently broken down since. In 1555 it was enacted that any parishioner who refused to make a suitable contribution should be "gently exhorted" by the parson and churchwardens, and if he was obstinate he should be sent for by the bishop and talked to. In 1563 it was recognised that even the eloquence of the bishop might fail; and it was provided that an "obstinate person" should be summoned before the Justices (or mayors in towns), who should lay an assessment upon him. And finally, in 1572, the Justices were empowered to make a direct assessment, and to appoint overseers of the poor to take charge of the whole business.

The relief of the poor thus fell under the supervision of the Justices. *Sed quis custodiet custodes ipsos?*—who would supervise the Justices? The answer is the Council. It is a very striking fact that until quite recent years England has been distinguished from the countries of the Continent in the possession of a systematic national provision for the destitute. And this is the more remarkable because England by no means led the way in this matter. It did but follow in the wake of the Low Countries, of

Economic Organisation

France and Germany. The principles involved had been clearly stated, among Protestants by Luther and Zwingli, among Catholics by the humanist Vives; they had been discussed and accepted by the highest theological tribunal of the western world, the Sorbonne; and they had attracted universal attention when they had been carried out by the enlightened municipality of Ypres. It is curious that one Flemish city, Ypres, should have led the way in the reform of the relief of the poor, and another, Ghent, should occupy the same honourable position in our own time with regard to unemployment insurance. But the continental poor-relief measures, for various reasons still rather obscure, did not succeed in permanently establishing themselves. The outcome was different in England, because here the Privy Council had sufficient hold upon the country to force the Justices to do their prescribed work. And, curiously enough, it seems to have been during the period 1629–1640, when Charles I tried to dispense with a parliament, and the Privy Council was quite exceptionally vigorous in dragooning the country gentry, that the Poor Law finally took firm root in English soil. The policy of "Thorough" was successful in this one direction, whatever it may have been in others.

These, then, were the main outlines of the Tudor system of government. It assumed that normally every able-bodied subject willing to work could find employment on satisfactory terms. This assumption was likely to be realised in a more or less static society; a society in which there was little change in the volume and distribution of employment, or in

Tudor Nationalism

which the changes were so gradual that the labour force could readily adjust itself to altered circumstances. But, as a matter of fact, the demand for labour was violently disturbed during the period in more ways than one. To begin with, it was seriously diminished in the country districts by the enclosures for sheep farming; "for one shepherd or herdsman," wrote Sir Thomas More in 1516, "is enough to eat up that ground with cattle, to the occupying whereof about husbandry many hands were requisite." For this reason, if for no other, the Tudor government could not hesitate to interfere and try to stop the enclosure movement. And it had two other reasons, which are clearly set forth in Lord Chancellor Bacon's *History of Henry VII.* Bacon's whole political attitude, be it noted in passing, was based on a consistent theorising of the Tudor policy; and, according to Bacon, enclosure was prejudicial alike to the king's revenue and to the king's military power. When, says he in the passage from which a few words have already been quoted, "enclosures began to be more frequent, whereby arable land, which could not be manured," *i.e.* worked or cultivated, "without people and families, was turned into pasture, which was easily rid by a few herdsmen; and tenancies for years, lives, and at will, whereupon much of the yeomanry lived, were turned into demesnes; . . . the king knew full well that there ensued upon this a decay and diminution of subsidies and taxes; for the more gentlemen, ever the lower books of subsidies." Moreover, "it hath been held," he continues, "by the general opinion of men of best judgment in the wars . . . that the prin-

Economic Organisation

cipal strength of an army consisteth in the infantry or foot. And to make good infantry, it requireth men bred, not in a servile and indigent fashion, but in some free and plentiful manner. Therefore if a state run most to noblemen and gentlemen, and the husbandmen and ploughmen be but as their workfolks and labourers or else mere cottagers, which are but housed beggars, you may have a good cavalry, but never good stable bands of foot. And this is to be seen in France and Italy, and some other parts abroad . . . inasmuch as they are enforced to employ mercenary bands of Switzers, and the like, for their battalions of foot."

Hence the several statutes to check sheep farming; and especially the most important of all, that of 1489, which prohibited the "letting-down" of houses of husbandry which were used with twenty acres of ground or upward. This, as Bacon explains, would serve, if enforced, for both purposes—to maintain a substantial yeomanry and to provide employment: "the houses being kept up did of necessity enforce a dweller; and the proportion of land for occupation being kept up did of necessity enforce that dweller not to be a beggar or cottager, but a man of some substance, that might keep hinds and servants and set the plough a-going." Hence a series of Royal Commissions of enquiry, beginning with one in 1517 of which Sir Thomas More was a member; with others in 1548, 1566, 1607, and then in rapid succession in 1632, 1633, and 1636. Here again the Council of Charles I tried to carry through a policy of Thorough in the teeth of enclosing landowners; and one of the reasons for the unpopularity of Archbishop Laud with the squirearchy was his vigour

Tudor Nationalism

ous efforts to "lay open enclosures." I cannot help thinking that the action of the government, spasmodic as it was, and apt to be hindered by the selfish interests, from time to time, of certain great lords on the Council (as in the minority of Edward VI), did do a good deal to check the enclosure movement.

But England was now becoming a manufacturing country as well as an agricultural one; and to the long-continued dislocation of agricultural labour was now being added the periodical depression due to fluctuation in the demand for manufactured goods. Occasional over-production is the inevitable concomitant of all manufacture carried on for a wide market, when there is not sufficient knowledge and concerted action among manufacturers to adjust supply to demand. We have seen that the woollen manufacture was the first, and for centuries the only, English industry to obtain a foreign market; we have seen that this extension of the market was in part the cause, and in part the effect, of the appearance of the new classes of capitalist middlemen, viz. the clothiers and of capitalist exporters, viz. the Merchant Adventurers. And as soon as a foreign cloth trade had been created, it began to suffer from grave periodical depression and lack of employment —due usually to a temporary loss of the foreign market owing to various causes, political or economic. The government was not inclined to look on passively; both because its whole social policy rested on the assumption that the willing workman could always get paid employment, and also because weavers out of work were apt to be turbulent and a danger to the public peace. And the policy of the Council was

Economic Organisation

precisely the same in this respect from the days of Cardinal Wolsey to the days of Charles I. In 1528, 1586, 1622, 1629, they did just the same thing. They sent to the Justices of the counties affected, and directed them to summon the clothiers before them and urge them to continue to give employment. Such measures are intelligible when we find that, in the time of James I, a really prosperous clothier—and there were many such—was reckoned to find work for some five hundred persons. "We may not endure," wrote the Council in 1622, "that the clothiers should, at their pleasure and without giving knowledge thereof unto this Board, dismiss their workpeople, who, being many in number and most of them of the poorer sort, are in such cases likely by their clamours to disturb the quiet and government of those parts wherein they live." The clothiers commonly replied that they could not find a market for their cloth at Blackwell Hall: the London merchants, they alleged—especially the Merchant Adventurers, who had a monopoly, as against other Englishmen, of the export cloth trade—would not buy from them. Thereupon the merchants were sent for and severely talked to, and threatened with the loss of their privileges if they did not take the accumulating bales off the clothiers' hands.

The fluctuation of employment was likely to be even greater under the domestic system than under the factory system. For under the latter the manufacturer has a strong motive—in his fixed plant, which would otherwise remain idle, and in the rent and rates and other general charges which must run on but little diminished — to keep his works going as long as

Tudor Nationalism

possible, and to manufacture for stock. But under the domestic system the clothiers had no works or plant to be kept going.

It was apparently deemed a reasonable answer to the remonstrances of the Council for the clothiers to point out that the merchants had ceased to take their goods. Could the merchants have done otherwise? Cardinal Wolsey evidently thought they could: "When the clothiers do daily bring cloths to your market for your ease, to their great cost, you, of your wilfulness, will not buy them." To behave so was to behave "not like merchants but like graziers"—a byword for selfishness in those days of enclosure. It is interesting to note how surprised statesmen were, or feigned to be, at the naked manifestation of commercial self-interest. Perhaps there was even then enough capital in the hands of the merchants to enable them to anticipate to some extent the reopening of the foreign market, temporarily closed by international complications; a little pressure from the Council may have been salutary. But it must be remembered that the exporters traded on their individual account: the only plan by which the risk of buying ahead of demand could be fairly distributed would be to raise a joint stock to which they should all contribute; and this was apparently done at least once, in 1586.

But, if it came to the worst, there was the Poor Law to fall back upon. "If there shall be found a greater number of poor people," wrote the Council to the Justices in 1622, "than the clothiers can employ, we think it fit, and accordingly require you, to take order for putting the statute in execution, whereby there is

Economic Organisation

provision made . . . by raising of public stocks for the employment of such as want work." This is an aspect of the Elizabethan Poor Law which is often left out of account. The Overseers of the Poor, ran the act of 1601—repeating legislation which went back to 1572—were to provide "a convenient stock of flax, hemp, wool, thread, iron and other stuff, to set the poor on work." The full history of this policy is still to be written. Perhaps the need diminished as time went on; but for half a century or more the parish authorities did, as a matter of fact, try in many places to provide work for the unemployed. The attempts were doubtless often ill managed and badly organised. We are not told how the parish authorities managed to dispose of the output; but, on the other hand, we certainly are not sufficiently acquainted with contemporary circumstances to condemn the Tudor policy off-hand.

LECTURE VI

Agricultural Estates and English Self-Government

IN this lecture I intend to deal with the distribution and cultivation of agricultural land in England during the centuries since the Revolution of 1688. We are compelled to take that starting point, though we should like to go further back, because we there get some sort of statistical basis in the calculations of the contemporary statistician, Gregory King. According to his estimate, there was then a population in England and Wales of five and a half millions. Out of these, more than four and a half millions, if we may trust his calculations, were still maintained by agriculture, and not half a million by manufacture and internal trade. Some three-quarters of a century later, Arthur Young, the celebrated author of the agricultural *Tours*, writing in 1769, estimated the population as being then at least eight and a half millions, and of these he ascribed hardly more than three millions to agriculture, and just three millions to manufactures. Neither of these estimates is likely to be very close; but if they at all approximate to the truth, they indicate not only a very great increase in the manufacturing population, but also a considerable decline, positive as well as comparative, in the rural population.

Economic Organisation

But 1688 is also, in itself, a date of the utmost significance for our present purpose. It marks the definite establishment of Parliamentary Government in England. Whatever power, for a century and a half to come, monarchs might continue to exercise, they had to obtain through their influence in Parliament. And Parliament reflected the interests of the landlord class, reinforced or mitigated, from time to time, as the case might be, by those of the merchants. It became impossible for an English monarch, even had he desired it, to pursue a policy not in line with the views represented in Parliament. Now the investigations of Knapp and his disciples have proved beyond a doubt that in Germany the maintenance of peasant cultivators over a great part of country was due, very largely, to the policy of "peasant protection" followed by Frederick the Great and other paternal princes of the eighteenth century. They insisted on the retention of the existing number of peasant holdings on the estates of the lords of land; and this for precisely the same reasons as Lord Chancellor Bacon, as we have seen, assigned for the measures of Henry VII. In their judgment, the absorption of the customary peasant holdings in the lords' demesnes was injurious both to the revenue and to the army. And, like the Tudors and early Stuarts, they fixed their attention on the keeping up, *de facto*, of the number of peasant households, and avoided the question of the legal right to the property. But with the fall of the independent power of the Council, nothing of this kind was any longer possible in England.

Moreover, in the years immediately preceding and

Self-Government

succeeding the Revolution in England, the crown lands passed almost entirely into private hands. Such a change was naturally favoured by political thinkers who wished the crown to lose all sources of supply outside Parliament. Yet it was precisely on the crown lands, more conservatively managed, as they commonly were, than other properties, that in more than one of the larger German states customary tenancies survived, right down to the time, towards the end of the eighteenth century, when governments came to be inspired by a pro-peasant policy and set about converting tenancies into ownership.

The course of English political development was confirmed by the ecclesiastical changes which accompanied or followed the Reformation. The country where to-day peasant proprietorship is most universal is perhaps Bavaria. There the Counter-Reformation was triumphant, and the Church retained its estates. And this contributed in the long run to the extension of peasant properties in two ways, negatively and positively. Negatively, because the unenterprising ecclesiastical lords allowed their customary tenants to remain ; so that, when, in the nineteenth century, Church lands were secularised, there was a body of cultivating peasants still in occupation who could easily be converted into owners. Positively, because the large subsidies which the sovereigns obtained from the ecclesiastical assemblies saved them from dependence on a parliament of squires. We have seen already how in England the dispersal of the monastic lands into lay hands under Henry VIII enlarged the area within which the ordinary motives of landlordship would be likely to operate

Economic Organisation

energetically. But it should also be noticed that the abandonment by Convocation in 1662 of the right of granting clerical subsidies was an important step in the process which finally deprived the English king of all chance of pursuing an independent social policy.

And now let us look more closely at the rural population in 1688. There can be little doubt that by that time the class of large landowners already occupied, at least in some districts, the position in which we now find them. What Lord Eversley calls "the ideal of the English land system" was already in large part realised. Sir Roger de Coverley, the baronet of Worcestershire described by Addison in the *Spectator* in 1711, was "landlord," he tells us, "to the whole congregation" in the parish church, as well as patron of the living. When the sermon is finished, the knight walks down from his seat in the chancel between a double row of his tenants, who stand bowing to him on either side. He "is a justice of the quorum; he fills the chair at quarter sessions with great ability, and three months ago gained universal applause by explaining a passage in the Game Act." He is, in fact, already "the squire" of English fiction—the squire of Fielding and Washington Irving, of Trollope and Mrs. Humphrey Ward. Yet the "ideal" of which Lord Eversley speaks was not yet by any means completely realised. There were many villages not yet dominated by a single great landowner; there were still a considerable number of small landowners—either freeholders or copyholders with a security of tenure amounting practically to complete ownership. These were the famous "yeomen" of England, at a time when "yeomen" was something

Self-Government

more than a picturesque literary term. There were, for instance, at least two of them among Sir Roger's near neighbours; and the Spectator came up with them as they were riding to the assizes: one is described as "a yeoman of about a hundred pounds a year," who "has been several times foreman of the petty jury;" and the other was left by his father fourscore pounds a year, but had lost so much in consequence of his litigious temper that he was not then worth thirty. With these figures of yeomen's incomes may be compared a passage which implies that the income of Sir Roger himself was at least £500 a year. How many such yeomen can we suppose there to have been, about this time? Well, Gregory King gives the following estimates: 160 temporal lords, with average incomes of £3200; 800 baronets, with average incomes of £880; 600 knights, with average incomes of £650; 3000 esquires, with average incomes of £450: practically all of these must have owned whole parishes, in many cases several parishes. Then King goes on: 12,000 gentlemen, with average incomes of £280: the contemporary use of the word "gentleman" implied the ownership of landed estate; 40,000 "freeholders of the better sort," with average incomes of £91; and 120,000 "freeholders of the lesser sort," with average incomes of £55. According to these figures, the total income of the lesser landowners was still almost five times that of the esquires and other large proprietors.

A century later—as we learn from Arthur Young, writing in 1793—"small properties" in England were "exceedingly rare"; and the general impressions we get from his writings have lately been confirmed

Economic Organisation

by statistical inquiries based upon the Land Tax Assessments. The amount of land in twenty-four Oxfordshire parishes held in properties of less than 100 acres diminished between about 1600 and 1785 by two-thirds; in ten Gloucestershire parishes by four-fifths; and much the same "consolidation of estates and shrinkage in the number of small owners" can be shown to have taken place over the rest of the country. If we may generalise from a few known cases, the building up of the very large estates proceeded most rapidly between about 1720 and 1785.

Now how did this take place? Mainly by purchase. This would be recommended to their employers by up-to-date stewards. The agent to the Duke of Buckingham, Edward Laurence, in a well-known treatise, *The Duty of a Steward to his Lord* (1727), advises the steward not to forget "to make the best enquiry into the disposition of any of the freeholders, within or near any of his lord's manors, to sell their lands, that he may use his best endeavours to purchase them at as reasonable a price as may be, for his lord's advantage and convenience." The small owners were offered prices in excess of the capital value of their properties as sources of income, and were glad to get the money to pay off their debts, put into trade, or even to stock larger farms as tenants. Where did the buyers obtain the purchase money they so freely offered? Mainly from wealth gained in trade. The last quarter of the seventeenth and the first quarter of the eighteenth century were marked by an extraordinary expansion of English oversea trade, as illustrated by the struggle over the privileges of the East India Company, so

Self-Government

graphically described by Macaulay, side by side with a great enlargement of the woollen industry, which furnished the chief article of export, and the establishment of new trades, especially silk-weaving, by the Huguenot refugees. It was the money made in trade which enabled the government to contract a great public debt, and it was in return for a loan that a body of public creditors were granted the privileges of a banking company and so created the Bank of England. A "moneyed interest," as the political writers of the time termed it, came into existence; or rather grew into so much larger proportions as for the first time to balance the "landed interest." To writers who clung to the ideals of the past it was a subject for lament that, in the language of Swift, "power which was used to follow land" had "now gone over to money." But owing to the peculiar character of English nobility, and the peculiar system of English government, it inevitably became the dearest wish of the moneyed interest itself to join the ranks of the landed, and there were no such obstacles in the way as existed in some other countries. Men enriched by trade bought estates and tried to "found families"; and men of old county families "married into the city," and strengthened their position in the country by the use of the fortunes of heiresses. Once obtained, great estates were kept together by the device of "Family Settlements." This requires some explanation.

In England there is now no such thing legally as "entail"; *i.e.* land cannot be indefinitely tied up in such a way, by any single deed or conveyance, that

Economic Organisation

its ownership must necessarily pass henceforward in a certain prescribed line. At one time, certainly, entails were authorised by the statute *De Donis* of 1285: according to that statute, land granted to a man and the heirs of his body could not be permanently parted with by the grantee, and after his death it necessarily passed to his lineal heirs. But, in course of time, means were found for evading the act; especially by the device of a fictitious lawsuit, called a "common recovery," which enabled the life tenant (or, as we should say now, the life owner) to free himself from the restriction, and obtain the right of selling or otherwise disposing of the estate. Taltarum's case in 1472 approximately marks the time when the contrivance was fully allowed by the courts. The great lords, including the king, might wish to secure the reversion of the estates they had granted to their vassals, by insisting that possession should be limited to descendants in the direct line, and that, when the line failed, the land should escheat to the superior lord; but the great body of the landed gentry were evidently too strong for them, and insisted on disposing of their lands as they pleased. It is the more remarkable that about the middle of the seventeenth century the process of legal construction should in effect be exactly reversed, and that legal ingenuity should be turned, and with success, to the invention of means by which estates, when once obtained, could be "kept in the family." An accurate account in any brief shape of the legal steps involved in a "strict settlement" is beyond the wit of man to compose: the whole business is immersed in a sea of technicalities

Self-Government

in which only lawyers, and but few of them, can swim with safety. But the effect of what happens is that by a series of legal arrangements, repeated in every generation, commonly at the marriage of the heir, the ownership of the estate is always settled for a generation ahead. Primogeniture is secured from generation to generation, and the nominal proprietor is never more than a "life tenant." "Primogeniture" indeed, as an authority has well said, who himself belonged to one of the Whig houses, "is accepted by the whole nobility, the squires of England, the lairds of Scotland, and the Irish gentry of every degree, as almost a fundamental law of nature, to which the practice" of settlement "only gives a convenient and effectual expression."

The credit for having added the last completing touches to the necessary legal procedure is ascribed to Orlando Bridgman, a famous conveyancer of the Commonwealth period, who became Lord Keeper under Charles II; and it is commonly supposed that the object of the device was to secure landed families from the forfeiture of estates during the troubles of the Civil Wars. It is curious to find that the arrangement known as "Fideicommiss," which in Germany achieves precisely the same object as the English strict settlement, though in a somewhat different way, is also traced to a contemporary and not dissimilar period, that of the Thirty Years' War. But while it was estimated, in the middle of last century, that in England the estates under settlement exceeded two-thirds of the kingdom, the *Fideicommisse* in Prussia, as late as 1895, only covered some six per cent. of

Economic Organisation

the area of the state, and even in Silesia did not amount to fifteen per cent. Of late years, however, their number has been growing so rapidly as to attract a good deal of attention. The explanation is to be found in the number of men who have recently acquired great fortunes in business and in finance, and who now seek to found country families for the sake of the social consideration, the sport, and, it would appear sometimes, the titles of nobility, which in a country like Prussia large landed estate is supposed to bring with it. The old aristocracy complain that "good old-fashioned landlordism suffers from the invasion of the Berlin Bourse," and cry out for a law which shall prohibit the formation of *Fideicommisse* by recent purchasers.

All this helps to explain the fresh vitality poured into the landowning class in England in the seventeenth and eighteenth centuries from the circles of trade and finance. For why did wealthy Englishmen seek to accumulate estates and then to keep them together? Partly, no doubt, because they were held to be peculiarly safe investments. But in new countries like America it does not occur to millionaires to create great country estates. The reason, as Toynbee pointed out, is to be found in the character of the contemporary political system. To begin with, landed estate of a sufficient size practically secured for its owner, if he was not quite exceptionally stupid or drunken, the position of Justice of the Peace. Such a position gave dignity and secured respect, as well as substantial power.

Gneist, the most distinguished German constitu-

Self-Government

tionalist of the last generation, wrote a famous history of the political system of England, to which he gave the title *Self-Government*. The very name implied praise; and it was meant by Gneist to indicate the superiority of the English administrative system, which he held up for the imitation of his countrymen, over the bureaucratic system of France. And his conception of "self-government" he thus defines: "internal administration of the country by unpaid magistrates, having control, for the purpose, of local rates." But this means simply that administration of the country by the Justices, and especially by the corporate authority of Quarter Sessions, which remained in their hands until it was taken away from them and transferred to elected County Councils in 1888. I remember when I was a student at Göttingen—some years before, but at a time when the inevitable change was already looming in the distance—hearing a lecture by the distinguished German historian, Reinhold Pauli. He ended his course on English constitutional history by giving a glowing account of the fabric of local government. But as we left the lecture room he said to me, "I haven't the heart to tell them that what I have been describing is passing away." And with all its great merits—merits in itself in spite of the jests about "Justices' justice," and, still more, merits as the alternative to a bureaucracy—the English system of local "self-government" was one of the main reasons for the desire to build up large landed estates.

The other main reason was the character of the central government,—the Parliamentary oligarchy. The power of the Whig ministry rested on the control

Economic Organisation

of votes in Parliament. Large landed property gave its owners great local influence in determining the elections. Those who controlled the elections could demand a share of ministerial patronage. And as the settling of estates left the younger sons of the landed gentry to be otherwise provided for, they must be quartered on the army, the church, and the public services. Large estates, local administration, parliamentary government, patronage, and primogeniture were thus all inseparably associated.

It should not be forgotten that it was not only yeomen, accustomed to put their own hands to the plough, who were induced to sell out. In certain parts of the country—and especially in the west, where the substantial village and widespreading manor of the Midlands had not been the rule—there were in the sixteenth and seventeenth centuries a considerable number of small landowners, who, whatever their origin may in reality have been, were accounted gentry by the heralds of the period, with the right to armorial bearings. In their Visitations of Devon between 1531 and 1620, the heralds enrolled fourteen "gentle" families whose names began with A, forty-seven beginning with B, sixty-three beginning with C. Of the A families only one remains among the landowners of to-day; of the B and C families only five under each letter. The rest have disappeared, and their lands passed into other hands, chiefly to new families coming out from the towns. And it is interesting to observe that, the more commercial England in fact became, the more general was the contempt for trade among the landed gentry who were themselves largely

Agricultural Estates

its offspring. It is probably with perfect accuracy that a well-known writer, who has an extensive knowledge of the genealogies and traditions of the west country, attributes the "irruption of false pride relative to 'soiling the hands with trade'" to "the great change that ensued after Queen Anne's reign." "Vast numbers of estates changed hands, and passed into the possession of men who had amassed fortunes in trade; and it was among the children of these rich retired tradesmen that there sprang up such a contempt for whatever savoured of the shop and the counting house." Certainly the Elizabethan and Jacobean monuments to be found in parish churches record the origin of many a squire's wealth in his prosperity as "Citizen and Mercer," "Citizen and Haberdasher," of London or some other town, in a way for which it would be hard to find parallels on the mural tablets of a later date.

But while actual purchase will explain the disappearance of a great many of the small separate properties, which were actually "freehold," and of those copyholds which were distinctly recognised to be "copyholds of inheritance," it does not account for the development of landlordship in another and perhaps even more important direction. It explains it extensively, but not intensively. We have seen that the result of the enclosures of the sixteenth century was not greatly to diminish the number of peasant families except in certain districts. Most of them had stayed on their customary holdings in much the same material condition as before; but with many of them a change had been effected in their legal status. They

Economic Organisation

had been induced to "surrender their copies," which so long as they retained them might perhaps have given them a secure heritable estate, in return for leases for lives or for terms of years. Fitzherbert concluded his well-known book on *Surveying*, printed in 1523, with a frank piece of advice and a remarkable prophecy. Let the lords of manors encourage the tenants to exchange their strips one with another, so that each may enclose "one little croft or close next to his own house," by offering to grant to each of them a lease at the same rents and services as before, "to have to him and to his wife and to his children, so that it pass not three lives, then being alive and named." " The lords, meseemeth, can do no less than to grant them these three lives of the old rent, remembering what profits they may have at the end of the terms, they know not how soon. For, undoubted, one set day cometh at last, and though the advantage of the lords come not anon, it will come at length. And therefore saith the philosopher: *Quod differtur non aufertur:* that thing that is deferred is not taken away." Some of the new owners of monastic lands were not inclined to be so patient. " Making us believe that our copies are void," the tenants are represented as complaining, "they compel us to surrender all our former writings, whereby we ought to hold some for two and some for three lives, and to take by indenture for twenty-one years." How far such extreme measures went we cannot say, but we have reason to believe that Fitzherbert's more moderate and cautious advice was frequently followed. A definite agreement that the lease should be renewed

Agricultural Estates

on the same terms, which was sometimes made, was not always complete security. Thus we know that on certain royal estates in Elizabeth's reign, the tenants accepted leases for forty years, renewable at the option of the holder, on payment of a fine of two years' rent, instead of their "copies and customary estates"; but when one of the estates was sold to the servant of a courtier they were in great alarm, "perceiving that they were likely to have their lands and tenements after the expiration of their leases taken from them." And well in the eighteenth century Laurence is heard teaching the same lesson to his readers as Fitzherbert: "Noblemen and gentlemen should endeavour to convert copyhold for lives to leasehold for lives."

Now all this does not mean that as soon as the leases expired, the holding at once became a yearly tenancy at a competitive or rack rent. As a fact the leases—especially of larger farms—were very commonly renewed time after time on payment of a lump sum known as a fine. In many cases the convenience of occasionally receiving a good round sum—especially where the landlord was a corporate body and the fine was divided among its members—was a powerful reason against converting the holding into a yearly tenancy. But the change from copyhold into leasehold, when there was no express right of renewal, had this effect: it turned the landlord into the absolute owner, with a legal right to dispose of the land as he pleased, instead of being a partial owner only, sharing the property in it with a tenant who enjoyed an heritable right—in other words, it

Economic Organisation

destroyed the semi-proprietorship of the peasant copyholder. It was sometimes asserted in the eighteenth century that leases for lives or for long terms of years, renewable on paying a fine, ought in justice to be regarded as constituting a certain tenant right: that the son or other representative of the previous tenant ought to have "a renewable right," even without express stipulation in the lease, on payment of a fixed fine. But this contention was never supported by the courts. And thus almost insensibly, as the result of a change from copy to lease which to very many tenants might seem purely formal, the old tenant-right passed away. Only a few copyholds, and they copyholds of inheritance, remained as exceptional curiosities; and no new tenant-right arose in England like that which managed to form itself in Ulster.

So much then for the ownership of land: the growth in extension of landed estates, and the intensification of the landlord's ownership within the several manors. We may suppose both to have gone on briskly during the first three-quarters of the eighteenth century. We have now to look at a second but closely connected series of changes—the amalgamation of farms. This was also one of the measures advised by Laurence in 1727: "the steward should endeavour to lay all the small farms, let to poor indigent people, to the great ones." But he recommends patience, and that the landlord should wait till farms fell in by death; and it seems to have been in the latter part of the century that the policy began to be generally carried out. When it came, it was the concomitant of the second and much more sweeping movement of en-

Agricultural Estates

closure; and this again was largely the consequence of a great wave of interest in agricultural science.

An enthusiasm for agricultural improvement took possession of a few great landlords early in the Hanoverian period. The pioneer was Lord Townshend, who about 1730 turned away with disgust from political intrigue and devoted himself to his estates. The great achievement by which he earned the honourable title of "Turnip Townshend" was the field cultivation of turnips and clover. This rendered unnecessary the customary triennial fallow, and so rendered possible the so-called Norfolk or four-course system of agriculture, which became the model for the rest of England; and which, by making it possible to keep stock in large numbers, increased the supply of manure and so resulted in richer crops. A little later, Bakewell in Leicestershire revolutionised the art of the grazier, and showed how the ox and sheep might be grown for food and not for draught and wool. As Townshend led the way in producing grain for the coming millions, so Bakewell produced beef and mutton for the millions. The oxen and sheep in the Smithfield market were from two to three times as heavy at the end of the eighteenth century as at the beginning.

Soon after the accession of George III, the passion for improvement became general among landlords. The way was led by Coke of Holkham, who possessed large means which he could devote to the enrichment of the soil and to the introduction of new crops and artificial cattle-foods on the farms he took into his own hands from tenants who refused to accept leases at increased rentals. His rent-roll increased from

Economic Organisation

some £2000 in 1776 to some £20,000 in 1816: but this was the result of a bold and lavish expenditure of capital, as well as of untiring personal application to the management of his estate.

The consequence of these and similar improvements all over the country was a vast increase in the production of food. And this increase rendered possible the expansion of our population, which was stimulated by the growth of the factory industries, offering employment to children, and by that most mistaken policy with regard to poor relief which was adopted generally by the Justices at the end of the eighteenth century, and which made it a paying speculation for the rural labourer to marry early. We are accustomed now to think of English manufactures as being exchanged for foreign food supplies: it must be remembered that well into the nineteenth century this could not take place. It was impeded no doubt to some extent by the protective tariff; but it was impeded also by the long Napoleonic wars; and even if the freest importation of corn had been permitted, there were no foreign supplies available to feed the rapidly growing English population until the virgin soils of the New World were made accessible, in the last quarter of the nineteenth century, by improvements in transportation. Indeed, during the worst years, when prices were at their height, from 1795 to 1802, importation under the operation of the sliding scale was, in fact, almost free. The English population certainly went through hard times: but it was at any rate kept alive, and enabled to increase fifty per cent. between 1750 and 1800 and a hundred per cent. between 1800 and 1850.

Agricultural Estates

Under these circumstances there was every motive to augment the productivity of the soil. The object appealed to the immediate self-interest of the landlords, since it would increase their rents; and it might well seem a patriotic duty, since it would find food for the growing population and enable England to resist the world domination of Napoleon. And what obviously stood in the way was the open-field system of farming with intermixed strips which still prevailed over perhaps half the arable area of most parishes in central and southern England. It was uneconomical and prevented improvement, and hence reformers like Arthur Young, who began his celebrated tours in 1767, were never weary of calling for its abolition, and with it of the common pastures. Enclosure had never absolutely ceased since Tudor times, but now it began again with fresh ardour; and between 1760 and 1850, by means of Enclosure Acts, practically all the remaining open fields and most of the commons were swept away.

We cannot doubt that the change was associated with a vast improvement in agricultural methods and in the production of food; and Jeremy Bentham, the utilitarian philosopher, had some justification in thinking the spectacle of an enclosure "one of the most reassuring of all the evidences of improvement and happiness." The high price of wheat in the later years of the eighteenth and the early years of the nineteenth century furnished both a stimulus and an excuse for the enclosure movement, just as the demand for wool had done in Tudor times; for wheat could be grown much more profitably on enclosed farms.

Economic Organisation

A chart which registers the number of enclosure acts and the price of wheat per quarter shows that they moved together : the higher the price, the greater the number of enclosure acts pushed through. And it seems to have been proved recently that the amount of injustice in the reapportioning of the rights involved was less than has often been supposed. The small open-field farmer, however, and still more the cottager were often more injured by the enclosure of the waste or common, inasmuch as it prevented his keeping cows or pigs, than by the throwing together of the acres in the open fields : and two-thirds in extent of the land enclosed was in fact common or waste.

The agricultural reformers of the time believed not only in enclosed farms but in relatively large farms. And here, as soon as the economists made their appearance in the first half of the nineteenth century, the agricultural writers had the supposed authority of political economy on their side. Farming on a large scale, it was supposed to be demonstrated, was more economical than on a small : its gross produce might not be greater, but its net produce certainly would be.

This was probably true enough for cereal farming, which made large wheat crops its main object. Accordingly, M'Culloch, the permanent economist of the *Edinburgh Review*, vigorously advocated large farming as the best means of promoting national well-being. " If a country were generally divided into small farms," he wrote in 1838, " a much greater number of labourers would necessarily be engaged in the cultivation of the soil, and there would be a proportionally smaller quantity of its produce to dispose of to others." While

Agricultural Estates

In France, he asserted, two-thirds of the people were employed in agriculture, in England less than one-third sufficed to carry on an infinitely superior system of cultivation. "Here is the powerful spring that has contributed more, perhaps, than any other to enable us to carry our commercial and manufacturing prosperity to its present unexampled height, and which makes us advance in the career of improvement. Let us not, therefore, by giving the smallest countenance to any scheme either for dividing estates or for building cottages on wastes, do anything that may tend to increase the purely agricultural population. The narrower the limits within which it can be confined, the better will be our agriculture, and the greater will be the surplus produce with which to feed the other classes, on whose numbers and prosperity the wealth, power and glory of the country must ever mainly depend."

The conjunction of the self-interest of the landlords who in the nineteenth century were mostly Tories, with the supposed science of the economists who were mostly Radicals, had the natural result. Small farms of twenty, thirty, forty, fifty and sixty acres were thrown together to form large farms of from a hundred and fifty to two hundred acres ; and on many a large farm of to-day the small farm-houses of an earlier period are still standing, divided into labourers' dwellings. And thus the large capitalist farm system which had arisen first on the demesne lands was extended finally to the lands once held by small customary tenants : and the social gulf between farmer and labourer was left bridgeless over the larger part of the country.

LECTURE VII

The Industrial Revolution and Freedom of Contract

"THE Industrial Revolution" has come to be the generally accepted designation for a certain period of English economic history. It owes its present vogue to its employment by Toynbee as the title of his lectures, published in 1884; and its place in economic literature has been confirmed by its adoption as the title of the elaborate and substantial treatise of a French scholar, M. Mantoux, two and twenty years later. The term was not absolutely original with Toynbee. Several years before, Jevons in the book on the *Coal Question* which aroused so much attention, had remarked in passing that "writers of the eighteenth century entertained most gloomy anticipations concerning the growing debt, and they were only wrong in undervaluing the industrial revolution which was then proceeding"; and it is highly probable that other writers had used the same descriptive term even before Jevons. Yet it was Toynbee's use of it which drove home the idea that the events of the period to which he referred did indeed involve a change so complete and so rapid as to be properly designated "a revolution."

With the term as Toynbee and Mantoux employ it, no fault can be found. But in this case as in others—

The Industrial Revolution

for instance, that of "the Renaissance"—the progress of historical science consists first in introducing emphasis and constructing large generalisations, and then in going on to readjust the proportions, and give due weight to qualifications. This is the more necessary because what to Toynbee and Mantoux was "the industrial revolution of the eighteenth century" has become in the mouths of their popularisers "*the* industrial revolution."

The qualification which now needs calling attention to is that the changes between, let us say, 1776 (when Adam Smith published the *Wealth of Nations* and James Watt perfected the steam-engine) and 1832 (the date of the first Reform Bill), did but carry further, though on a far greater scale and with far greater rapidity, changes which had been proceeding long before. No great period is in actual fact sharply cut off from that which precedes and follows it; and for our present purpose it is perhaps more important to view the development in the reign of George III as a culmination of movements already on foot than as creating something entirely new.

The primary force that was at work was Capital, and the capitalistic spirit—the desire of Investment for the sake of gain—which was bound up with it. Long before 1776, by far the greater part of English industry had become dependent on capitalistic enterprise in the two important respects that a commercial capitalist provided the actual workmen with their materials and found a market for the finished goods. The workmen continued to work in their own homes or in sheds or outhouses attached to them; and for this reason

Economic Organisation

the system may be spoken of as *domestic*, (German: *Hausindustrie*). I think this is on the whole the most convenient practice, and I have followed it in the previous lectures. As it happens, however, the term *domestic system*, when it was first used in England, in the 1806 Report of a Committee of the House of Commons, was applied to somewhat different conditions. It was applied especially to the organisation of the woollen industry in Yorkshire; where the cottage manufacturer bought his own wool and then got it spun for himself, and hence was no mere wage-earner, but the producer of a commodity which he himself sold to the merchants at the cloth hall or otherwise. Some of the witnesses sharply distinguished this system from the system of the West of England, where the workman never owned the material and therefore never owned the goods, and was simply paid wages by the clothier who employed him. The same distinction between cottage manufacturers selling their product and cottage workmen selling their labour is to be found in the industrial history of other countries, and French and German writers have made various attempts to invent a suitable terminology. In German the word most commonly used for the latter conditions is *Verlagsystem*. *Verleger* is a term still in common use for a merchant who gives out work to be done in the employé's own workshop or workroom: the English term which most nearly covers the same meaning is *factor*. *Verlag* is the building whence material is distributed and where the finished goods are stored: *warehouse* is perhaps the nearest equivalent. I remember that when I was wandering once around

The Industrial Revolution

the "small forge" district of the Thuringian forest, a smith looked up from his anvil to ask me if I was the *Verleger* from the neighbouring town. If we are to invent a new term, perhaps *factor-system* might serve; although the employing capitalists in England were only in certain small trades actually called "factors." *Commission-system*, which has been proposed, is obviously inaccurate, because the work was not done on commission, either by the employing capitalist or by the cottage workman.

A good deal of discussion, too, has turned upon the relation between the two forms of organisation, and between each of them and what preceded and followed. It has been argued that it is mistaken to group them together; that "the domestic system" of Yorkshire, and forms like it, were really more closely akin to the handicrafts of an earlier period: the difference consisted simply in its diffusion over rural districts, and the disappearance in Yorkshire (and commonly in similar cases elsewhere) of the gild organisation binding the several master craftsmen together. On the other hand, "the system of the clothier of the west of England," like similar arrangements in other trades and other lands, where the cottage workmen were simply wage-earners, has been said to be more closely akin to the factory system. In this case the manufacture itself, it is urged, had become capitalistic, and not simply the "merchanting" part of the business: and the factor-system, leading to production on a large scale—large from the whole industry though not in the individual shop—and supplying a wide national or even foreign market, was merely an earlier stage of

Economic Organisation

that *grande industrie* of which the factory is the later form.

The difficulty is that, though cases may actually be found which do indeed answer well enough to these characterisations, they are not sufficiently universal to serve the purposes of classification without a good deal of caution. To begin with, the difference between being paid a price for goods sold and being paid a wage for work done may in practice almost disappear, so far as either the sense of independence or the material well-being of the workman is concerned. And the total output of an industry working under the former conditions and the market ultimately reached by it through various capitalist intermediaries, may be—and in the Yorkshire case actually were—very considerable.

The question of classification and terminology, however, so far as England is concerned, may be passed over with some equanimity because in the period between the gild and the factory it was that more completely capitalised form which involved the provision of material by the capitalist and the payment by him of wages which was by far the most widely prevalent. That this was the case with the clothiers of the south and west of England throughout the sixteenth and seventeenth centuries is beyond all question. The rising woollen trade of Yorkshire instead of being typical in this respect was exceptional; and, in consequence perhaps of the subsequent concentration of the woollen industry in the West Riding, and the picturesque description by Defoe, it has been assigned a larger relative importance than it deserves.

The Industrial Revolution

To that I shall return: the point I want just now to emphasize is that the plan of giving out material and paying wages was characteristic of every other important industry in the eighteenth century. The proof is to be found in the legislation against embezzlement of material. If we turn to the article "Manufacturers" in Postlethwayt's two great folios, *The Universal Dictionary of Trade and Commerce,* published in 1755, we shall find that it sets forth "the principal laws of England relating to manufacturers and artificers," and that these are concerned entirely with this characteristic evil of the prevalent system. There was first the temporary act of 1702, reciting that "many frauds are daily committed by persons employed in the working-up of the woollen, linen, fustian, cotton and *iron* manufactures, by embezzling and purloining of the materials with which they are entrusted," and providing certain penalties. In 1710 it was made perpetual. The act of 1740 extended its provisions to persons employed "in cutting or manufacturing gloves, breeches, leather, boots, shoes or other goods." This "proving deficient," in 1749 the workpeople affected were classified anew, as "any person hired to make any felt or hat, or work up any woollen, linen, fustian, cotton, iron, leather, fur, hemp, flax, mohair or silk manufactures." In all these cases the dominance of the capitalist middleman was due to the fact that, as things then were, he was needed to organise the manufacture and to assume the risk which was involved in advancing the necessary capital, in view of a market which was too distant and uncertain for the individual artisan to cope with. The craftsman was

Economic Organisation

not yet necessarily "divorced from the instruments of production"—to use the phrase of certain modern writers: he commonly owned his own loom in the woollen and silk trades, just as many a sweated sempstress of our own day owns her own sewing-machine. It was not the instrument of production, but access to the market that he was cut off from by circumstances. And the essential similarity between industrial conditions then and under the subsequent factory system is shown by the fact that we already come across combinations of cottage workpeople against their merchant employers and movements for higher wages.

Before going further we must pause for a moment to consider the exceptional conditions in the cloth industry of the West Riding. Those conditions are thus described by the Report of 1806: "The manufacture is conducted by a multitude of master manufacturers, generally possessing a very small and scarcely ever any great extent of capital. They buy the wool of the dealer; and in their own houses, assisted by their wives and children, and from two or three to six or seven journeymen, they dye it (when dyeing is necessary) and through all the different stages work it up into undressed cloth. . . . The manufacturer" then "carries it on the market day to a public hall or market where the merchants repair to purchase. Several thousands of these small master manufacturers attend the market at Leeds, where there are three halls for the exposure and sale of their cloths; and there are similar halls at Bradford, Halifax, and Huddersfield." And like similar small manufacturers elsewhere, we are further told that "a great proportion of the

The Industrial Revolution

manufacturers occupy a little land, from three to twelve or fifteen acres each."

Three questions suggest themselves: first, why did capital play this relatively minor part in Yorkshire, when in the production of woollen goods of much the same kind (*i.e.* "woollen" as distinguished from "worsted") it was so much more prominent elsewhere; second, how were the goods marketed; and third, how long did these conditions survive. To the first question, the answer is probably that the capitalist mercantile clothier did not make his appearance in Yorkshire until some considerable time after the industry had risen to importance in that county in the seventeenth century, because the West Riding was a relatively poor district, far behind the fertile counties of the south in agricultural wealth, and a long way off from the capitalists of London and Norwich. Capital did not come forward because in that district it did not exist. To the second question the answer is given by the public markets. In the beginning these were in the open air; on the bridge at Leeds and then in Briggate, at Huddersfield alongside the churchyard. Then, as the numbers increased who frequented the market, covered halls were provided: in Leeds in 1711, in Halifax and Wakefield a year or so before. When the domestic industry was at its height, from 1750 to 1780, every town of any size in the district erected from one to three spacious buildings of this kind. Such meeting-places for merchants and manufacturers, where goods could be gathered together and displayed, were necessary features in domestic industry of this type; and the buildings of this sort still standing in many

Economic Organisation

localities of western Europe testify to its former prevalence. Here the smallest manufacturer, who could bring in only one piece a week, could spread out his cloth on the boards with as good a chance to dispose of it to the merchants who came thither as his most prosperous rival. On the third question, how long such conditions lasted, a good deal of light has been thrown by the recent publication of some letters of a Halifax cloth-factor for the year 1706. It is clear that, as early as this, no small part of the business of exchange was being taken away from the public market. Cloth merchants had established permanent connections with particular makers, and now gave them direct orders. Moreover, there was a class of agents or factors, giving orders on commission either for London merchants or for merchants of Rotterdam, Amsterdam, and Hamburg, and making little use of the public market. And when, under the first two Hanoverian sovereigns, the worsted manufacture, hitherto the monopoly of the Norwich area, was introduced into the Bradford district, the new branch of business was almost from the first carried on by men of larger capital, resembling more nearly the clothiers of the west country. For this two reasons have been assigned which would seem to be adequate : the materials were more expensive and needed more capital for their purchase, the work was less difficult and required less skill on the part of the weavers and the other operatives. Capital took control and operative skill became subservient.

From this digression let us return to the general English movement. Conditions approached more nearly to the later factory system when the capitalist

The Industrial Revolution

"undertaker" owned the necessary instrument of production and let it out to the workman—as, for instance, in the hosiery industry with its knitting-frame. There has been a great deal of discussion as to the distinction to be drawn between the "tool" and the "machine": the one, it has been said, can be owned by the workman, the latter is too expensive. If this distinction is valid, then the handloom and the knitting-frame, like the sewing-machine of to-day, were midway between the two. They were not beyond the means of some workpeople: but they were relatively so expensive that under certain circumstances there was an opportunity for a capitalist to step in and supply them.

An even closer approximation to the factory of later days would be reached when the capitalist thought it expedient to gather a body of workpeople together in one place, under one roof. An organisation of this kind Karl Marx christened "manufacture," as distinguished from the factory system dependent on machinery; and he laid down that it was "the prevalent characteristic form of the capitalist process of production throughout the period from the middle of the sixteenth to the last third of the eighteenth century." The word "manufacture" was certainly not limited in England, during that period, to this particular sense, and it would be difficult to introduce it now as a technical term: but the name would not matter if the fact were as Marx stated. But it is equally certain that though occasional examples may be found, as in the pin manufactory described by Adam Smith, the aggregation of workpeople under the control of capitalists was not the "prevalent characteristic" of the period. That is surprising, both

Economic Organisation

because something of the kind can be found in the English woollen industry in the first half of the sixteenth century, and because what may seem like a case can be made out for such a stage in continental development.

John Winchcombe of Newbury, who died about 1520, and soon became legendary as the greatest of English clothiers, was said by later tradition to have employed a hundred looms in his house. Another rich clothier, soon after the dissolution of the monasteries, is reported by an eye-witness to have filled every corner of the lodgings of Malmesbury Abbey with looms, and he was in negotiation for the buildings of Osney Abbey for a like purpose. Moreover, the Weavers' Act of 1555 complains that certain clothiers had set up divers looms in their houses and worked them by journeymen and unskilful persons. Why these experiments were given up it is impossible at present to say. We can hardly explain their abandonment by the act I have mentioned, which forbade any weaver *outside a town* to have in his house or possession more than two looms, or any "person using the feat or mistery of cloth making"—*i.e.*, I presume, any clothier—also outside towns, to have more than one. The act remained on the statute book as late as the beginning of the nineteenth century, and the Committee of 1806 reported that "it is highly valued, and its repeal strongly opposed by a very respectable class of petitioners." But this could not have prevented such establishments being set up in the market towns, like Tiverton, where in fact most of the clothiers lived. We may conjecture that it was

The Industrial Revolution

the policy of the Tudor government to frown upon undertakings of that kind : for an act of 1585, relating to a coarse cloth made in Cornwall and Devon, exclusively for the Breton market, expressly limits the number of looms in that business to three in one house, whether in town or country. But whether it was legislation which brought them to an end or simply the discovery that such aggregations were after all not particularly profitable, and that more could be made with the same capital in commerce overseas, phenomena of this kind did altogether disappear from the woollen industry and the other staple trades until a very short time before the introduction of machinery.

During the Stuart period, it is true, large works were established from time to time for various manufactures. Among these were glass, soap, and wire. Their history has still to be written : but the very fact that it is obscure shows that they could not have flourished to any very large extent. And in the next century the similar attempts made in the staple trades were few in number and evidently not particularly successful. There is an interesting passage in one of Arthur Young's *Tours* describing what he found in Yorkshire in 1768. At Boynton, he says, " Sir George Strickland was so obliging as to shew me his woollen manufactory ; a noble undertaking, which deserves the greatest praise. In this country the poor have no other employment than what results from a most imperfect agriculture ; consequently three-fourths of the women and children were without employment. It was this induced Sir George to found a building large enough to contain on one side a row of looms of different sorts, and on the other a large space for women and children to spin. The undertaking was once carried so far as to employ a hundred and fifty hands, who made very sufficient earnings for their maintenance; but the decay of the woollen exportation reduced them so much, that now those employed are, I believe, under a dozen."

In attributing so much importance to "manufacture," in the special sense he assigned to it, Marx would seem to have been generalising from France. The "manufactures royales," which were large establishments enjoying special governmental favours in the way of subsidies and exemptions from taxes, and the "manufactures privilegiées," which were similar establishments enjoying a monopoly of certain branches of the trade, are said between them to have turned out at one time two-thirds of the cloth produced in France: and in other industries similar establishments had a like period of success. But all the advantages enumerated by Marx as flowing from co-operation in labour would not have succeeded in establishing these "manufactures" without the active support, and even in many cases the initiative, of the government. This was one of the great achievements of Colbert. When the government withdrew its assistance, the "manufactures" at once began rapidly to decline; and it seems very doubtful whether their existence vitally affected the subsequent development of industry. In England, the efforts of the government in this direction under the early Stuarts were wrecked by the outcry against monopolies: under the later Stuarts the monarchy was not in a position to carry out a strong industrial

The Industrial Revolution

policy of its own, and there was no minister like Colbert to attempt it.

Without special governmental favours, the advantages which the collection of his workpeople in a single building would give an employer were usually too slight and too dubious to encourage any large movement in this direction. Where the work could be broken up into a number of separate operations, as in the manufacture of pins, it would doubtless greatly facilitate that type of division of labour to bring together under one roof a sufficient body of men for each to be assigned a specialised job. But where, as in the woollen industry, division of labour could not go beyond the processes of combing, spinning, dyeing, weaving, fulling, &c., there would be no such gain in a mere aggregation of workpeople, performing the same operation. The only advantages that I can discern would lie in the better supervision of the quality of the work and in the greater regularity of output. Against these had to be set the cost of providing the building as well as of the necessary supervision. Accordingly the only successful introduction of the textile factory, on a considerable scale, before the last quarter of the eighteenth century, was in the silk-spinning industry; and here the explanation is to be found in the introduction of machinery which required "power" (in this case supplied by water) beyond that producible by human muscle. It is only because the spinning of silk was, after all, a relatively small trade that the advent of the factory on the Derwent in 1718 did not transform English industrial life as the subsequent cotton factories did.

Economic Organisation

The appearance of the factory is therefore the characteristic feature of the industrial revolution of the later years of the eighteenth century, even though it had actually come into existence sporadically half a century earlier. It meant a new forward step in the evolution of capital: the assumption, on a large scale, by the owner or controller of capital of a further function besides that of the mercantile intermediary—the function of actually directing and supervising the manufacturing process itself. And this, if it did not produce absolutely new phenomena, immensely intensified the effects of the capitalist control already established. The effects, I hasten to add, were good as well as bad. For the advent of capital brought about a vast enlargement and cheapening of production. This should never be lost sight of, though it is so obvious that one sometimes forgets it.

The cotton "factory" was so much the most striking example of the new conditions, that "factory system" is on the whole the most expressive term to describe the new organisation. But of course the essential feature of the phenomenon is the aggregation of a body of workpeople in one workplace, drawn together by the necessity of attendance upon power-machinery, and directed by capitalist employers. This was to be seen in the coal-mine and in iron or engineering works just as much as in the textile factory. Undoubtedly it was the necessary outcome of the great mechanical inventions. Of these there may be distinguished two parallel series— one in the textile sphere and one in the allied spheres of coal, iron, and steel. I do not propose to give an

The Industrial Revolution

account of them : it is easily found in many a book. It is well to bear in mind in studying them what Jevons has remarked as to the three conditions of invention. There must be, first, the discovery of a new principle for the accomplishment of some mechanical task. That principle may be discerned centuries before the idea is actually realised, because the other two conditions are absent. Secondly, a method of construction must be invented by which the principle can be carried out. And thirdly, a strong practical purpose must present itself, for which the new mechanism is urgently needed. Thus in the history of the steam-engine, the business motive was furnished by the desire to get rid of the water which began to trouble coal miners as shafts became deeper ; and in the textile series, the business motives were, first, the desire to get abundant cotton yarn in order to supply the recently improved handlooms, and then the desire to improve the loom still further in order to make rapid use of the now cheapened and abundant yarn. Throughout, the growth of population, and the improvement of transportation (by turnpike roads, canals, and later by railways), accompanied the progress of manufactures. It is impossible to say that either was simply the cause or the effect of the others. All three stimulated and promoted one another.

Recalling what we have already seen as to the function of capital while industry was still in the "domestic" or "factor" stage, it is clear that its assistance would be even more necessary when machines had to be purchased and works erected. Besides Jevons' three pre-requisites, there was, accordingly, another

Economic Organisation

which had to be realised before manufacture could pass into the machine era: viz. the provision of capital. The manufacturer might conceivably borrow it: in our own day, as we all know, manufacturing activity, as well as mercantile, is greatly forwarded by the organisation and extension of credit, through banks and discount houses. In the Industrial Revolution also this factor must be assigned a share: for it is significant that country banks, which had previously been very few in number, increased quite rapidly from about the time of the American war; and Adam Smith closed his chapter on banking by a paragraph designed to show that "the late multiplication of banking companies, by which many people have been much alarmed," was all for the best. Competition, he argued, would compel them to be "more circumspect," while it would also "oblige all bankers to be more liberal in their dealings with their customers." But while overdrafts might supplement capital, and the discounting of bills might enable manufacturers to turn over their capital more quickly, they would not actually provide, in the first instance, the requisite resources. The mechanism of the limited liability company, by which capital is contributed both by shareholders outside the actual management and also in the form of debentures or bonds, was, of course, in 1776 three-quarters of a century away.

Ricardo and the "classical" economists, therefore, were simply giving expression to the facts around them when they wrote as if the men who directed manufactories were themselves, as a rule, the owners of all or almost all the capital they made use of, and

The Industrial Revolution

when they started the habit, which has survived till to-day, of speaking as if the capitalist and the employer were necessarily the same person. Even in 1848 John Stuart Mill observed that "the control of the operations of industry usually belongs to the person who supplies the whole or the greatest part of the funds by which they are carried on."

We have still to explain the self-owned capital of the earlier generations of factory owners. And recent discussions of this question have taken us back with a renewed appreciation to the phrases of contemporary economists. "Capitals," says Adam Smith—and it is instructive that he uses the word in the plural—"are increased by parsimony and decreased by prodigality;" and he contrasts the unproductive expenditure of the rich on "idle guests and menial servants," with "the maintenance of productive hands" "by what a frugal man annually saves." Senior, in 1835, introduced the term "abstinence," as more fitly expressing the source of capital. All that his argument required was the purely negative sense which makes abstinence mean simply non-consumption; yet he characterised abstinence as implying "self-denial," and declared that "to abstain from the enjoyment which is in our power" is "among the most painful exertions of the human will." Phrases like these have occasioned no little mirth : it is hard to discover self-denial or parsimony, as the world understands those words, in the processes by which modern capital is most largely accumulated. But as applied to the beginnings in the eighteenth century of modern manufacturing capital, the terms are exact and appropriate. To a great extent it was

Economic Organisation

in actual fact the result of "parsimony" and "abstinence," as the plain man uses the words.

That the new manufacturing middle class was largely Nonconformist is a very familiar fact. But what have not been sufficiently noticed are the economic consequences in the eighteenth century of Nonconformist conceptions of religious duty. I need not now discuss how far those conceptions were due to the individualism of their theology, an individualism which in Calvinism and later religious movements had gone a good deal beyond the individualism of the earlier stages of the Reformation : nor how far it was due to the political and social circumstances in which the Dissenters found themselves. Whatever may have been the causes, certain ideas became dominant among them, which had not indeed been altogether absent from the Christianity of earlier centuries, but had then been moderated in their operation by other and conflicting opinions. Among these ideas we may single out the following : business as a divine "calling"; the sinfulness of pleasure-seeking; the lawfulness of material gain. "If God," replied Richard Baxter in 1673 to the enquiries of his congregation, "shew you a way in which you may lawfully get more than in another way, if you refuse this and choose the less gainful way, you cross one of the ends of your calling, and you refuse to be God's steward." Pecuniary means, acquired by assiduous application to business and the prudent choice of the gainful way, naturally accumulated when there was no expenditure on amusements or on interests outside the business, the family, and the religious "connection." To a shrewd and scru-

The Industrial Revolution

pulous observer like John Wesley, this was a matter for grave alarm. "Religion," he wrote, "must necessarily produce both industry and frugality, and these cannot but produce riches. . . . We *must* exhort all Christians to gain all they can and to save all they can : that is, in effect, to grow rich." "But as riches increase, so will pride, anger, and love of the world." The only remedy in his opinion was for "those who *gain* all they can and *save* all they can" to "likewise *give* all they can." It is not uncharitable, however, to conjecture that, with ordinary humanity, the natural way to dispose of savings, which could not be used for display or self-indulgence, was in business investment. And here we have doubtless the explanation to a large extent of the way in which capital was found in middle-class business circles to finance the new inventions.

The establishment of the factory system would inevitably have been attended by great social dangers and difficulties even if the social situation had been altogether satisfactory in every other respect. In the closing years of the eighteenth century and the opening years of the nineteenth, this was, I need hardly say, by no means the case in England. There was the great war which involved heavy taxation; and there was a recently elaborated system of out-door Poor Relief which, however benevolent in intention, was in actual working exceedingly demoralising. But let us concentrate our attention on the industrial position. We have there to deal with two absolutely different sets of facts. There was, first, the effect of the competition of the new machine-made goods with similar goods made by hand. The supersession of a

Economic Organisation

widely extended handicraft by mechanical methods of production involves a problem which no country so far has had the wisdom to solve satisfactorily: in England it was the long-drawn agony of the handloom weavers (when the new machinery, first applied to the rising cotton trade, was introduced into the deep-rooted and widespread woollen industry) which added so greatly to the gloom of the Chartist period. And secondly—and it is this that specially concerns us here—there were the conditions produced within the machine-using industries themselves. In all of them the cost of the machinery necessarily created a wide social cleavage between employers and employed. Although what we may call "patriarchal" conditions of intimacy and mutual knowledge survived far more than is commonly supposed, and survive even to-day, the personal tie tended to be replaced, wherever large bodies of workpeople were brought together, by a purely "cash nexus." This was not, as Carlyle might lead us to suppose, due to any peculiar hardness of heart on the part of the employers: it was due to the necessities of the situation. And as the personal tie weakened, employers were likely to press more strenuously their right—and even, as they might urge, their duty—to be governed by profit-making considerations, and to be more intent on buying their labour as cheaply as possible. The absence of combination among the workpeople put them at a disadvantage in their bargaining for remuneration; while the like absence of combination among employers forced the more benevolent among them to follow the lead of the more "business-like." Meanwhile, in the

Freedom of Contract

textile industries there were even graver immediate causes of evil. The new machinery rendered the work physically so light that it became possible to employ women and children in large numbers; and the sinking of capital in costly machinery made it seem the interest of employers to work that machinery as continuously as possible. Neither the employment of children nor excessive hours were absolutely new phenomena. Both had been seen in the domestic workshop. But the employment of children was now systematised and extended on a vast scale; and excessive hours, instead of being an occasional episode, say once a week, became a regular thing, every day in the week.

The country was the slower in dealing with the situation because of what had now come to be the prevalent belief, not only in business circles but also in the minds of the intellectual leaders of public opinion, that control or regulation by the State was an antiquated and irrational policy; that the State ought to limit its functions to the maintenance of what was called "law and order," and that the liberty of the individual to pursue his own interest in his own way—what was denominated "freedom of contract" —was not only socially expedient, but also a natural right. It is interesting to observe how in this matter the pressure of business interest went side by side with the elaboration of an abstract social theory. For a century after the Revolution of 1688, the Whig party, which found its theoretic justification in John Locke's doctrine of natural rights, was also the party of the mercantile or moneyed interest. And this interest,

Economic Organisation

though it demanded protection and privilege in foreign trade, found the existing State regulation of industry at home very much in its way. Listen to the frank utterances of Sir Josiah Child, the great East India merchant, in his celebrated and oft-reprinted *Discourse of Trade*, first published in 1698:

"All our laws that oblige our people to the making of strong, substantial (and, as we call it, loyal) Cloth, of a certain length, breadth and weight, if they were duly put in execution, would, in my opinion, do more hurt than good, because the humours and fashions of the World change, and at some times, in some places (as now in most), slight, cheap, light Cloth will sell more plentifully and better than that which is heavier, stronger and truer wrought; and if we intend to have the trade of the World, we must imitate the Dutch, who make the worst as well as the best of all manufactures, that we may be in a capacity of serving all Markets and all Humours.

I conclude all our laws limiting the number of Looms, or kind of servants, and times of working, to be certainly prejudicial to the Clothing-Trade of the Kingdom. . . .

I conclude that stretching of Cloth by Tenters, though it be sometimes prejudicial to the Cloth, is yet absolutely necessary to the Trade of England, and that the excess of straining cannot be certainly limited by any law, but must be left to the Seller's or Exporter's discretion, who best knows what will please his Customers beyond the Seas."

The period of Whig supremacy has been appropriately christened the period of "parliamentary Col-

Freedom of Contract

bertism." Its objects were the same as those of the strong paternal government of Louis XIV under his great minister Colbert; but the policy was shaped, not as in France by the independent, if mistaken, views of the crown and its chosen advisers as to the well-being of the nation as a whole, but by the immediate interests of the mercantile classes as expressed through Parliament. Unlike the Tudor policy, it fixed attention on the foreign market, on imports and exports, and allowed the whole system of internal regulation—justices' assessments of wages, apprenticeship, supervision of processes, &c.—to fall into abeyance. And when Adam Smith, continuing and developing the individualism which characterised all the philosophic speculation of the eighteenth century, turned the argument for individual liberty directly against the prevailing commercial restrictions, he did not hesitate to be consistent and denounce the surviving remnants of industrial restriction at home as also contrary to the principle of natural liberty. Starting with the well-known Whig doctrine of Property as set forth by Locke, the philosopher of the Revolution settlement, he gave it an industrial application, à propos of the law of apprenticeship. "The property which every man has in his own labour, as it is the original foundation of all other property, so it is the most sacred and inviolable. The patrimony of a poor man lies in the strength and dexterity of his hands; and to hinder him from employing this strength and dexterity in what manner he thinks proper without injury to his neighbour, is a plain violation of this most sacred property. It is a manifest encroachment upon the

Economic Organisation

just liberty both of the workman and of those who might be disposed to employ him."

Under the influence of this belief the whole Tudor code as to wages and employment was swept away in 1813 (wages) and 1814 (apprenticeship). "The reign of Elizabeth," said the member in charge of one of these bills, "though glorious, was not one in which sound principles of commerce were known."

In a very few years the country began once more to build up again piecemeal a new industrial code, controlling the free play of individual action even more effectively than the code of Elizabeth. I have not time to enter into the details of the factory legislation by which England, as it preceded the rest of the world in its industrial evolution, set an example also for the rest of the world in coping with some of the gravest evils it produced. Let us indicate simply the leading stages. The hours of labour of children and young persons in cotton mills were limited in 1819; in 1833 this restriction was extended to all the textile trades, and a beginning was made in the creation of a staff of Inspectors to see that the acts were enforced. The Central Government, through the departments then existing or subsequently created of the Home Office, the Board of Trade, the Local Government Board, and the Education Office, resumed the task of enforcement of a social code which had dropt, a century and a half before, from the hands of the Stuart Council. In 1842 the State proceeded to interfere with the labour of adults, by excluding women from underground mines. In 1844 women were included with children and young persons in the limitation of factory

Freedom of Contract

hours. Those who advocated the measure did so with the knowledge that it would, in effect, limit the hours of employment of adult men in textile mills, and promoted it with that purpose—"fighting," as was said, "behind the women's petticoats." But the legislature did not take the next long step and directly regulate the hours of labour of adult men for almost half a century; until in 1893 it made a fresh departure by permitting the Board of Trade, on representation to it of excessive hours worked by railway servants, to bring a certain very gentle pressure to bear on the railway companies to revise their time schedules. Fifteen years later, in 1908, it took the gigantic step of limiting the number of hours to be worked by all underground coal miners; and this measure had been delayed so long only because the miners themselves had not been altogether unanimous in its favour.

Meanwhile, as early as 1844, the State had begun to enforce certain regulations with regard to safety by insisting on the proper fencing of machinery. Twenty years later, in 1864, the legislature proceeded to empower the Secretary of State to issue special rules regulating processes in dangerous trades; but again these were designed only for the protection of women and children, and it was not till thirty years afterwards that power was given, in 1895, to impose special rules in regard to workshops in which men only were employed. It is true that since 1850 the inspection of coal mines had been undertaken by the State, and every great catastrophe has since been followed by new rules to promote safety; and as early as 1875, freedom of contract as between seamen and shipowners had been limited by the enactment of the Merchant Shipping Act, which prohibited the loading of ships beyond the Plimsoll line : but these invasions of the responsibilities of employers were long regarded as altogether exceptional, and as justified by the peculiar helplessness of men who leave the surface of the solid earth to go down into its bowels or to traverse the sea.

Looking back on the history of the century 1813–1913, it is now evident that the development of industrial legislation has taken place chiefly in two periods. These are, first, the period of bitter struggle over the Factory Acts. In this struggle the economists were, as a body, in favour of freedom all round—in industry as well as commerce. The leaders of the Free Trade movement, and especially John Bright, strenuously opposed the proposed Factory Acts as "contrary to all principles of sound legislation." Sir Robert Peel, the son of a Lancashire cotton spinner, who became the idol of the free-traders, was the *bête noir* of Lord Shaftesbury, the champion of the cotton operatives; and the great Ten Hours' Act of 1847 was passed by the Tory country gentlemen, partly from honest conviction, and partly in revenge for the repeal of the Corn Laws by the representatives of the manufacturing interests in the previous year. But by 1850 the main lines of factory legislation were settled. Henceforth, for many years, the movement was of the nature of a very slow and cautious extension of its principles to industries allied to the textile group and to non-textile factories and workshops. During this period, when the principle of commercial free trade was accepted by both great political parties, it was also a matter of

Freedom of Contract

general agreement that freedom of industrial contract should be the general rule, and any "interference of the State" altogether exceptional: the presumption was held to be against it. And as it happened, the most formidable of the critics, from the historical side, of the individualist philosophy of the economists, Sir Henry Maine, in his work on *Ancient Law*, published in 1861, seemed to put the principle of free contract on an even firmer basis than before by representing it as the inevitable outcome of an age-long historical evolution. *From Status to Contract* came in to supplement *Laissez Faire*.

It was not till the 'nineties that really large new departures began to be made. The difficulties of Irish land tenure had opened the eyes of the political party which had been most closely identified in the past with the principle of individual liberty to the necessity of interfering with free contract between landlord and tenant at least in Ireland; but the old Political Economy could hardly be "banished to Saturn" in the case of Ireland without losing some of its vitality in England. Moreover the movement of European thought which, starting from Locke, had made men in the eighteenth century regard the State as a mere constable, whose only duty was to keep the ring within which individual competitors should fight out their battles, had, long before this, taken with Hegel another turn. Among the English thinkers who gave expression to a more trustful view of the State may be specially mentioned one who deeply influenced many of the young men who afterwards came to the front—the Oxford philosopher Thomas Hill Green. In a

Economic Organisation

modest pamphlet printed in 1881 he drew a far-reaching distinction between "mere freedom from restraint" and "freedom in the higher sense—the power of men to make the best of themselves." In this latter sense, freedom might actually be forwarded by greater restraint.

At one time it seemed as if the influence of Herbert Spencer's writings would bring fresh strength to the declining forces of individualism. But Spencer's antipathy to State action was hard to reconcile with his view of society as an organism, and went to extremes which robbed him of the support of practical men. Somewhat more effect was produced by Darwinism; it was seriously argued by certain devotees of science that because "the struggle for existence" led to "the survival of the fittest" in the biological sphere, no restraint of any kind should be laid upon economic competition. But here, again, the doctrine involved too complete a reversal of modern civilisation to carry weight with legislators: and it was never accepted by Darwin's effective populariser, Huxley. And when the period of stagnation in economic thought passed away, which followed upon the mid-century domination of Mill, and a new and more fertile period began, Jevons in 1882 broke away from the traditional presumption in favour of *Laissez Faire* and declared that every case must be considered on its merits.

Whatever the causes may have been, the last quarter of a century has seen the enactment of a great code of compulsory insurance: insurance in fact, though not in name, against Accidents, by the Workmen's Compensation Act of 1897, and, both in fact and name, by the In-

Freedom of Contract

surance Act against Sickness of 1911, and the measure coupled with it of insurance against Unemployment, at present restricted to three great trades, but doubtless soon to be extended to the whole field of industry. At the same time, as we have already seen, a fresh beginning has been made with the State regulation of wages by the Trade Boards Act of 1909 and by the Minimum Wage Act for miners of 1912. If the spirit of Burleigh, the great statesman of Elizabeth, could have heard what was said in the Commons when the legislation of his mistress was swept away in 1813-14, and could then have listened to what was said in the same chamber in 1908-12, he would have smiled with a grave satisfaction.

But historical evolution never really returns upon itself; there is always a vital difference between new and old, however much they seem to resemble one another. The difference between the Tudor situation and our own consists in the advent, meanwhile, of democracy. The State which has enacted the great measures of the last two decades is a democratic State, working mainly through paid officials; and that brings with it dangers just as real as, though different from, those involved in a monarchical State compelled to act through a landed aristocracy.

It is, I believe, a mitigation of those dangers that the modern State, in the matter of wages at any rate, can to a large extent make use of corporate organisations representing both sides of the wages contract. The years which saw the beginnings of State intervention saw also the first efforts of the workpeople to help themselves by substituting the "collective bargaining"

Economic Organisation

of trade unions for the impotence of the isolated workman. In earlier centuries combination among workmen to obtain an increase of wages had been forbidden by the common law because it was deemed to be the business of parliament and the justices to regulate the conditions of employment. When the governmental regulation of wages had, in fact, passed away, it might have been supposed that combination among workpeople would have been permitted. On the contrary, in 1799 combinations amongst workpeople were prohibited by statute. This law was repealed in 1824-25; but the very Radical who brought about its repeal did so in the expectation that "if left alone combinations would cease to exist." Combination long remained under the ban of the economists: to them it was wrong, because it was a violation of natural liberty, an interference with the freedom of each individual to make what bargains he pleased for himself; and it was also futile, according to the orthodox doctrine of wages. From Free Traders of the Manchester school it received no sympathy: "combinations," said John Bright as late as 1860, "must in the long run be as injurious to the working man as to the employer." Yet, as we all know, trade unions succeeded in establishing themselves in all the staple industries of the country, not without bitter struggles, in which there was often violence and folly on one side as well as ignorance of human nature and short-sightedness on the other. And by 1894 the Royal Commission on Labour was able to report that in the staple trades of the country there were "strong trade organisations which are accustomed to act together in masses, and have made the old method of settling

Freedom of Contract

individual wages by the haggling of the market impossible, and which have for the most part already caused the substitution for it of Wages Boards, or other more or less formal institutions, by which they secure a consultative voice in the division of receipts between capital and labour." "The most quarrelsome period of a trade's existence," the Commission remarks elsewhere, " is when it is just emerging from the patriarchal condition in which each employer deals with his own men with no outside assistance, but has not yet fully entered into that other condition in which transactions take place between strong associations fully recognising each other." And the great engineering strike of 1897-8, which raised the question of collective bargaining in a peculiarly difficult form, ended in an explicit recognition of that principle by the victorious employers in the terms of settlement.

It would be absurd after the upheavals of 1911 and 1912 to pretend that even the general recognition of the principle of collective bargaining will altogether solve the labour question. Even if the two sides come together and are ready to bargain on behalf of their constituents, they may not be able to reach an agreement. In this case a chairman or umpire—in the last resort appointed by the State—may have to decide, if the two parties can be induced to give him this authority. But he will be greatly assisted by previous discussion ; and his decision would be in vain unless there existed on each side organisations which could carry his decision into effect. In spite of recent storms the situation is really far more hopeful than it was when the combination of the workpeople was

Economic Organisation

actually far weaker; and the remedy would seem to lie, in part at any rate, in the direction of an even completer combination of the parties concerned. There are grave difficulties to be overcome before the problem is solved of the most suitable organisation on either side. Just now it is the question of trade union structure that is uppermost: whether it shall follow the lines of "crafts" (*i.e.* single industrial processes), or "occupations" (*i.e.* groups of kindred processes), or "industries" (as indicated by the grouping of employers). Probably no uniform solution will ever be possible; nor to the like difficulties on the side of employers. But this need not prevent the adoption of working arrangements which will be sufficiently effective for practical purposes. The industrial organisation of the future will probably emerge, as did that of the later Middle Ages, from a union of State regulation from above with spontaneous combination from below.

LECTURE VIII

Joint Stock and the Evolution of Capitalism

WE have seen that the establishment of the factory or "works" system implied the advent of large Capital in the field of manufacture, and the acquisition by its owners or users of the control over the whole process of production as well as of distribution. And it is obvious that what may conveniently and for brevity be called "Capitalism," *i.e.* modern methods of production directed for the profit-making purposes of capital, has in one respect been vastly successful. Human labour has been applied in an incomparably more effective way than before; science, by means of costly machinery, has utilised forces of nature to an extent and of a kind before undreamt of. Commodities in consequence have been inconceivably multiplied and cheapened; and, as a result, a population almost four times as great was supported on English soil in 1901 as in 1801, and in a state of material comfort which, for the great body of the people, was undoubtedly superior to that of a century before. But it is equally obvious that, human nature being what it is, the capitalistic organisation of industry under private ownership necessarily brought with it a certain opposition of immediate interests between employers and employed, and a constant risk of industrial conflict.

Economic Organisation

This being so, it was natural that lovers of their kind should look round for some way out of a troublesome situation. One idea that occurred to them was that the advantages of capital might be retained—the employment of machinery, and production on a large scale—but its disadvantages avoided if the ownership, in the case of each factory or works, could be achieved by its own workpeople. It was, in short, the remedy of Co-operation, as Co-operation was understood by those who first applied it to production. Its ideal was the self-governing workshop, eliminating the individual "employer" with his "profit," and thus abolishing "the wage-system." Encouraged by some apparent successes in Paris and London, in 1848 and the following years, John Stuart Mill predicted Co-operation's ultimate triumph. "The form of association," he wrote in 1852, in the second edition of his widely-read textbook of political economy, "which, if mankind continue to improve, must be expected in the end to predominate, is not that which can exist between a capitalist as chief and workpeople without a voice in the management, but the association of the labourers themselves on terms of equality, collectively owning the capital with which they carry on their operations, and working under managers elected and removable by themselves." Ten years later, in 1862, Mill declared that the experience already attained "must be conclusive to all minds as to the brilliant future reserved for the principle of co-operation." "It is hardly possible to take any but a hopeful view of the prospects of mankind, when, in two leading countries of the world, the obscure depths of society contain simple working men

Evolution of Capitalism

whose integrity, good sense, self-command, and honourable confidence in one another have enabled them to carry these noble experiments to a triumphant issue." The success of co-operation, he added, three years later, would bring about "a moral revolution in society; the healing of the standing feud between capital and labour; the transformation of human life from a conflict of classes struggling for opposite interests to a friendly rivalry in the pursuit of a good common to all; the elevation of the dignity of labour; and a new sense of security and independence in the labouring class."

But these anticipations have been grievously disappointed. Hundreds of experiments have been made, and there is a noble story to tell of persistence and self-denial in the scraping-together of capital; but undertakings for co-operative production in Mill's sense have without exception failed completely, either from the business or from the co-operative point of view. Some would have failed from stress of circumstances however well managed, but most of the failures were due to mismanagement. The undertakings either did not secure competent managers, usually because they were not ready to pay sufficiently high salaries, or else they quarrelled with them. Industrial self-government proved altogether incompetent to organise production and (what is even more important) to secure a market. Success, where it did come, was equally fatal; the small societies of handicraftsmen, such as most of the early co-operative groups really were, became exclusive if they were successful, and began to employ outside labour; the large societies formed

Economic Organisation

later in the cotton-spinning industry became mere joint-stock companies, in which, indeed, working men held shares, but in which the employers and employed ceased to be identical bodies. Capitalism has not, as a fact, been seriously modified by Co-operation. What is called Co-operation has had any considerable measure of success only in the sphere of retail distribution; the large manufacturing establishments run by the federation of distributive stores—the Co-operative Wholesale Society—are carried on in precisely the same way as any well-managed "private" business.

What is known as "Profit-sharing" differs from Co-operation in that it proposes to provide all (or, in its latest phase, "Labour Co-partnership," almost all) the capital otherwise than by the contribution of the workers in the several businesses, and to retain, in the hands of those appointed by the owners of the capital, the control over the management of the business. It proposes, however, to add to the wages of the workpeople some share of the profits, when profits are obtained over and above what is regarded as a proper interest on capital and a proper remuneration for management. Whether this be but a slight modification of the ordinary capitalist system or contain within itself the germs of a true co-operative system need hardly be discussed here, in view of the fact that hitherto its history, like the history of Co-operation itself, has been a record (in every direction save one) of repeated failure. The cause of failure in almost every case, from that in 1875 of Messrs. Briggs, of whose experiment Mill wrote in the most hopeful spirit, to that of some recent much-discussed proposals, has been the

Evolution of Capitalism

apparent incompatibility of profit-sharing with trade unionism. That incompatibility shows itself even when the concern which introduces the scheme does not make—as most of the earlier profit-sharing arrangements made—abstinence from joining a union a condition precedent to the sharing in profit. Employers have now to reckon with the fact that in any industry which employs skilled workmen under substantially similar conditions in a number of establishments, the workpeople of the several concerns are sure to be drawn together by a sense of solidarity of interests, and will certainly endeavour to promote what they deem to be their interests by joint action. Profit-sharing or Labour Co-partnership can hardly be worked without tending to detach the group of men employed in the particular concern from the general body of the trade. For that reason it is certain to be opposed by intelligent trade union leaders. There is only one industry in which it has been found possible to keep it alive hitherto, and that is the gas-making business. Following the precedent of Sir George Livesey and the South Metropolitan Gas Company, companies controlling more than half the capital invested in the gas business in the United Kingdom have introduced some element of profit-sharing. But this is a business in which the labour employed is almost entirely unskilled, and trade unionism has hitherto been very weak, and which is carried on under other conditions exceptionally favourable to profit-sharing. Chief among these are the large degree of local monopoly necessarily enjoyed by the several concerns, and also the peculiar system of legislative regulation to which the industry is subject,—a system

Economic Organisation

which makes an increase of dividend dependent on a reduction of price to the consumer, and so obviously and closely associates the interests of shareholders with the efficiency of the labourers.

So long as these conditions are absent from other industries, the only application of the idea of profit-sharing which would be feasible would be some plan which made the workpeople share in the profit of the whole industry to which they belonged, without regard to the fortunes of the particular concern by which for the time they were employed. But even then the difficulty would remain which has been felt in profit-sharing as applied to particular works, viz. that the principle that profit should be *shared* does not in the least determine *how* it should be shared. There is no general abstract principle that can be invoked from either side to evade the troublesome necessity of bargain between the parties concerned.

In opposition to the co-operative school, the great French philosopher, Auguste Comte, maintained—in the same year, 1848, as saw the initiation of co-operative undertakings—that "the division" which had "arisen spontaneously between Capitalist and Workmen" was not a thing that could be reversed. On the contrary it was to be regarded, he held, as "the germ" out of which a future and more satisfactory organisation of industry was to arise. The true solution of the difficulty, he declared, was that "the spiritual power," which he hoped to create, should "penetrate the employers with a strong and habitual sense of duty to their subordinates." As it was easier, he thought, to influence large employers in this direction

Evolution of Capitalism

than small, the "tendency to a constant enlargement of undertakings" was not to be lamented but welcomed.

Comte's hopes, then, were fixed on the "moralisation" of employers. It cannot be denied that some improvement has taken place in that direction. The first generation of factory owners included many overbearing and narrowly self-seeking natures: there is certainly now a far stronger sense prevalent of what employers owe to their workpeople. There has been a quickening of the employers' conscience; and to this the State by its factory legislation and the pressure of the workpeople themselves through their unions have both contributed in no small measure. And yet the vast change that has taken place in business organisation since Comte's time has evidently tended towards weakening even further the personal tie between employer and employed, and towards putting fresh obstacles in the way of any policy on the part of employers which aims at anything besides commercial profit. My reference of course is to the introduction of the limited liability joint-stock company, for which the English date is 1862. The joint-stock method has facilitated the provision of capital for business purposes beyond all expectation: but it has inevitably still further depersonalised the relations of labour and capital. Moreover, it has made the situation far more difficult in other ways. Directors feel themselves to be trustees for the shareholders, and morally bound, as such, to sacrifice philanthropy to gain. And owing to the unrestricted transference of shares, high real profits seem but modest returns to shareholders who have come in later and paid high prices for their stock

Economic Organisation

(simply because dividends were high), not to the company, but to the previous owners; so that, however large the trading profit may really be, the pressure of all those shareholders who have bought at a high price tends to be against anything that may possibly reduce it. The prospect of any moralisation of individual employers or single employing concerns resulting in a voluntary sacrifice of profit for the benefit of workpeople is very small under a joint-stock régime. What, in this position of affairs, is really more possible to hope for, is that profit-seeking itself should lead great manufacturing concerns to adopt measures within their works which will both benefit their people and directly (through internal economies) or indirectly (through the force of advertisement and appeal to the fellow-feeling of the consumer with the workman) accrue to the employers' benefit. There is room for much to be done in this direction—the direction not of self-sacrifice but of enlightened self-interest. Yet "welfare" programmes, to be permanently successful, must be so carried out as to be consistent with the independence of the workpeople, both political and economic.

Looking back then on the nineteenth century, we see that no fundamental modification has taken place in the organisation of industrial production. It has continued to be characterised by the dependence of large bodies of workpeople on the provision of capital by investors, induced thereto by the motive of profit. All that state action and labour combination have been able to do, in those branches of manufacture in which they have been effective, is to raise somewhat

Evolution of Capitalism

the plane of competition by enforcing certain standard conditions of employment. What accordingly we have now to observe is the evolution of capitalism, moving in accordance with its own internal laws.

This evolution has taken precisely the same road in England as in the other great manufacturing countries of the world. Its movement has been marked by four characteristics—(1) Concentration, with larger employment of fixed capital in proportion to labour, and greater average aggregation of workpeople—so that the actual number of mills or works increases more slowly than the number of employés; (2) Integration; (3) Combination and (4) Collective Action in the face of labour. Let us look at each of these separately.

First as to Concentration. On this head we have not yet for England any such easily accessible figures as are provided for Germany and the United States by the official census. There still survive in this country widespread industries, such as that of tailoring, not yet organised on factory lines, but conducted on the lines of the "domestic" industries of the eighteenth century. There are even a number of small handicrafts retaining many of the characteristics of the old gild industry, though the gilds themselves have long ago passed away. Moreover, new industries are continually coming into existence which in their earlier stages can be carried on successfully in small workshops. The factory system has not yet won the complete dominance which was prophesied for it half a century ago. Nevertheless, in the staple industries of the country, the factory or large "works" is the predominant form of organisation; and these works or factories become

Economic Organisation

steadily larger and more expensively equipped. Thus in 1844 the total capital invested in cotton mills and machinery was calculated at about twice the annual wages bill; in 1890 at five times the wages bill; the average number of spindles per mill and looms per mill was also at least fifty per cent. greater at the later date. And this was in an industry which has notoriously moved much less rapidly in the direction of concentration than some of the other staple trades, notably the iron and engineering group, and this because a cotton mill still costs comparatively little to erect and equip. Thus it has been reckoned that while there were about four times as many blast-furnaces in 1900 as in 1800, the average "make" per furnace had increased wellnigh fifteen times. It should be noticed, however, that this increase in the average size of plants, with a decrease or at any rate not a proportionate increase in their number, is not necessarily the same thing as a concentration in the ownership of the capital involved. Thus the number of breweries fell from forty-four thousand in 1850 to between five and six thousand in 1903; but with the conversion in the late 'nineties of brewery firms into joint-stock companies there went a wide diffusion in the holding of stock, so that at the later date the share- and debenture-holders in five alone of the largest brewery companies numbered some 27,000 persons. About the same time the capital in the English Sewing Cotton Company belonged to some 12,000 owners, in the Fine Cotton Spinners to between 5000 and 6000; while Lipton's great business had as many as 74,000 shareholders. It has indeed been argued that the diffusion of property

Evolution of Capitalism

in joint-stock undertakings is less than has sometimes been supposed, because a man of means commonly holds shares in several concerns; and some evidence has been adduced in support of the estimate that the owners of joint-stock properties do not number in all more than 500,000. But when one reflects that most of these must be adult males, usually with several persons dependent upon them, even this minimising estimate shows how far industrial capital is from being owned exclusively by millionaires. The industrial middle class now takes new forms; it now consists largely of officials of companies and holders of stock. But any one who has walked through the residential suburbs of our great manufacturing cities knows that it shows no sign of disappearing, in spite of the prophecies of Marx and his school. It may be doubted whether it was ever relatively stronger than to-day.

The second characteristic of capitalistic evolution, especially in the last quarter of a century, has been Integration. This has been peculiarly marked in the iron, steel, engineering, and shipbuilding group of trades. By Integration is meant the bringing under a single business control of a whole series of operations contributing to a final result which had been previously conducted entirely apart: for instance, of the whole of the operations involved in the making and employment of steel, from the mining of the ore and coal, through the blast-furnace and steel plant up to the production of hardware, machinery, or ships. In this direction the way was led by Carnegie in America and Krupp in Germany; but in the 'nineties England rapidly made up the leeway it had lost, and a dozen or more

Economic Organisation

gigantic unifications took place—either in the shape of actual amalgamation or by means of the purchase of controlling interests. Thus John Brown & Co. of Sheffield, owning coal mines, ore fields, blast-furnaces, and steel plants, and turning out armour plates, boiler plates, and a whole series of steel materials, amalgamated with the Clydebank Shipbuilding Company, which built battleships and turbine liners. Armstrong and Co. at Newcastle, beginning with making steel and ordnance, bought up a great engineering business and a large shipbuilding concern, and got a controlling interest in a famous locomotive and marine engineering works, and in the chief company of torpedo manufacturers. About the same time the great concern of Guest, Keen & Nettlefold in South Wales and Staffordshire brought under one management collieries, ore deposits, blast-furnaces, steel plants, and a whole series of manufactures of such products as nuts, bolts, and screws. These are but typical examples. In such integrating movements the initiative may come from either direction; it may start from the relatively finished manufactures, reaching back to get a secure hold upon their materials, or from the earlier stages in production, reaching forward to get a more secure outlet for their product. In either case the result is the same.

The third feature of capitalistic evolution—and again it has characterised especially the last quarter of a century—has been the tendency towards monopolistic Combination among concerns engaged in the same manufacture. "Monopolistic" I use in no necessarily bad sense, but simply to indicate that the main purpose of such combinations is to affect price by controlling

Evolution of Capitalism

supply. As there is no inherent sacredness in competition, and prices determined solely by competition have often been disastrous to the best interests of the workpeople engaged, there is no need to start at the word "monopoly." The promoters of a combination often, indeed, put forward "the economies of combination" as their motive, with the resulting advantages which they make possible to the public. In most cases this is only a very subordinate motive in actual fact; the real motive is the higher price which absence of competition may of itself be expected to render possible. But it must be acknowledged that economies by no means inconsiderable may often be obtained. Competitive trading is in several ways, especially in the expenses of advertisement and sale, an unnecessarily costly method of satisfying public wants; so that it is quite possible for a monopoly to result, at the same time, in a decrease of cost to the consumers and an increase of profit to the producers.

Combination in Great Britain has taken one of two forms—either that of an agreement, or the completer form of a complete amalgamation. Of the former, one of the most interesting is the agreement which controls the manufacture of steel rails; and this because it rests upon an international alliance among the steel makers of the United States, England, Germany, Belgium, France, and Russia, each national combination being given a monopoly of the home market and an allotted share of the rest of the world. A similar international agreement is now to be found in the tobacco business, and also, with occasional breaks, between North Atlantic steamship

Economic Organisation

lines. Of the latter type, the amalgamations, the chief examples are to be found in what are called "Associations," but are really completely amalgamated companies, created in certain branches of the textile industries between 1898 and 1900. These are very considerable concerns. Thus, the Calico Printers' Association has a capital of $8\frac{1}{4}$ millions sterling, the Fine Cotton Spinners of $7\frac{1}{4}$, the Bleachers of $6\frac{3}{4}$, the Bradford Dyers of $4\frac{3}{4}$. In each case the amalgamation now controls the whole trade. All of them, it will be seen, are subsidiary to the main textile processes—spinning and weaving; and it is significant that while all the chief subsidiary industries are now syndicated, the main body of each of the two great textile trades, that composed of the spinning and weaving branches, still remains subject to an almost unlimited competition.

It used to be believed by some who disliked both Trusts and Protection that England was effectually defended, as they put it, from trusts by its policy of free trade. But though England has hitherto remained a free trade country, it is no longer quite devoid of trusts. It is undoubtedly true, whether it be regarded as an advantage or no, that the commercial policy of this country has somewhat retarded the formation of trusts and rendered them less secure. But there are other important factors in the problem, and chief among these are the technical requirements of efficient production. With the increasing costliness of modern plant, competition is continually at work to reduce the number of competing firms. As soon as an industry comes to be carried on by a few very large

Evolution of Capitalism

concerns, it is easier for those concerns to come to an agreement; it is less likely that one of the parties to the agreement will break away, and an increase of price consequent upon the agreement is less likely to call new competitors into the field. When twenty firms made steel rails in Great Britain no agreement was permanent; now that the number has been reduced to nine, they apparently find it easy to hold together. As soon as the number of concerns in a trade can be counted on the fingers, they are likely to see their interest in alliance rather than in competition. And even moderate secure gains are coming to be preferred to the chances of competition. The nerves of the business world are growing weary of the strain of competition, and the human craving for security is one of the chief forces that are transforming industrial organisation.

When the trust is safe within the country itself, the risk of competition from abroad depends largely on geographical position. It is out of the question when the work is necessarily attached to a locality—like Manchester bleaching and Bradford dyeing. And where competition is still possible, there is increasing likelihood, in the present stage of affairs, that it will be warded off by international agreements.

A recent writer has drawn up a list of some eighteen large amalgamations or combinations of a monopolistic character—controlling, that is to say, each of them, the sale and price of some one important commodity or group of commodities. This is without reckoning the Railway and Shipping Conferences by which competition is removed from rates to facilities

Economic Organisation

and conveniences. But the custom of contrasting monopoly with competition has for some time been thoroughly misleading. It is not the case that, outside the visibly complete monopolies, competition still reigns unrestricted. The fact is rather that over the whole of the industrial field there is now a movement away from unrestricted competition to some greater degree of stability. It seldom culminates in absolute monopoly, but absolute competition will soon be even harder to find.

Moreover, the methods by which the way is prepared for combination by the reduction of the number of rivals, and by which the remaining rivals, on coming to terms, are able to prevent encroachment from outside, are the methods of competition itself. The Lord Chancellor, Lord Halsbury, in the famous Mogul case in 1891, which established the legality of the rebate device of the shipping rings, remarked that "if this is unlawful, the greater part of commercial dealings, where there is rivalry in trade, must be equally unlawful." Monopoly, that is to say, in restricting competition, is not relying on authority *ab extra*, like the state monopolies of the Stuart period: it is beating down competition with competition's own weapons.

In my judgment the marked tendency in recent decades towards the restriction, or even abolition, of competition is no ephemeral outcome of antisocial forces. The emergence of the trust is just as "natural" as the rise of the gild or the factory. It results from the inherent striving of capital towards profit; it proceeds from the good side of humanity, the impulse toward mutual assistance and the desire

Evolution of Capitalism

for stability, as well as from the less attractive side, the pursuit of gain. I am convinced that to future generations the era of unrestricted competition, with its recurring crises, will seem like a malady of childhood. I view the combination movement with the more hope because I regard the regularisation of production as the best hope for the labouring classes, for whom steadiness of employment is far more important than the amount of remuneration. But it is obvious enough that combinations, with all their possible advantages, involve certain positive risks for the consumer. Not so great as some people hastily suppose; for limits are put by self-interest even to monopoly prices; still risks considerable enough; and I have no sort of doubt that the State will be compelled after a time to step in and subject monopoly prices to a certain public supervision and, if need be, control, just as the English State already sets limits upon the charges of railway companies. What we have to do is to see to it that the modern State is as competent as may be to discharge its delicate but ultimately unavoidable task.

The remaining feature in the recent development on the side of capital is the growth of the feeling of solidarity among employers and the steady strengthening of their organisations for collective action in relation to labour. The great example of this is the Federation of Engineering and Shipbuilding Employers. Again and again in the past the workpeople have been better combined than the employers, and have won their battle by tackling them singly. It is lamented by some that that time is now passing away; that not only will

Economic Organisation

the employers in one trade throughout the whole of a district in future all stand together, but that the whole body of employers in each great industry all over the country will be so firmly knit together by a sense of community of interest as to have a corporate opinion strong enough to prevent even a great district, let alone a single concern, from making terms to suit itself. Just as at an earlier stage the coalowners of Durham would not permit individual collieries in the county to yield to trade union pressure without the consent of the other owners, so in a later stage the Glasgow employers in the engineering business maintained a lock-out long after they were ready themselves to grant their own men the terms asked, in order to maintain unity of action with the employers of Belfast. Undoubtedly this solidarity of employers' interests does for the time put greater difficulties in the way of trade unions in the realisation of their immediate objects. But it is apparently not only the natural response to a like tendency on the side of labour, but also, in many cases, the necessary preliminary for any further progress in the direction of industrial peace. As the difficulties in the docks of London made clear only two years ago, the great obstacles in the way of industrial peace are not only the extremists on the labour side, but also the employers (often comparatively small employers) who refuse to be bound by an employers' agreement to which they were not individually parties.

Society is feeling its way, with painful steps, towards a corporate organisation of industry on the side alike of employers and of employed ; to be then more harmoniously, let us hope, associated together—with the

Evolution of Capitalism

State alert and intelligent in the background to protect the interests of the community. The world has never yet had complete individualism; it will never, I believe, have complete socialism, for the egoistic sentiment is as permanent an element in human nature as the social. It has to create a working compromise suited for each age; and we are also beginning to realise that the old antithesis, which Herbert Spencer in his *Man v. The State* exaggerated into an antagonism, no longer exhausts the possibilities of the situation. A place must be found in our social organisation, and therefore in our social theory, for the activity and mutual relation of groups, of divers kinds and scales and degrees of compactness, intermediate between the individual and political government. This is the valuable thought to be discerned amid the excesses of Syndicalism; and this is the lesson of that newer philosophy of social organisms which is based, as by Gierke, on the study of history

APPENDIX

SUGGESTIONS FOR FURTHER READING

THE purpose of the following notes is neither to indicate the character and extent of the original sources of information nor to provide a bibliography of the modern literature of economic history. Their object is simply to inform those who are entering upon the study where they will find the several subjects dealt with, more or less competently, in the English language, and in a readable and not too technical manner. Many of the works referred to, it will be seen, have appeared since these lectures were delivered; and it need hardly be said that their conclusions are not to be regarded as necessarily authoritative, though always worth considering.

It should be remembered throughout that there is a vast amount of information, over the whole range of English economic history, to be found in Archdeacon Cunningham's *Growth of English Industry and Commerce* (1903, 1905). A few references will be given to the present writer's *Economic History* (originally published in 1888 and 1893). This was published in England as two parts of Vol. I. and in America as two vols., and will be here cited as *Econ. Hist.* i. and ii. Of i. the last edition should be used.

LECTURE I

The beginning of all real understanding of mediæval agricultural life is to be found in Seebohm's *English Village Community* (1883). The student cannot do better than start with the first 104 pages of that great work, where the author, beginning with a nineteenth-century map of his own township of

Economic Organisation

Hitchin, traces the main features of open-field agriculture through the documents of the Middle Ages back to the time of the Domesday Survey. Whatever may be thought of Seebohm's own theories, set forth in the later chapters of that book and in his subsequent *Tribal System in Wales* (1895) and *Tribal Custom in Anglo-Saxon Law* (1902), as to the origins of mediæval serfdom, subsequent enquiry has only confirmed the picture which he drew in the *English Village Community* of the conditions to be explained.

The most impressive statement of the theory that the manor grew out of a free self-governing village community will be found in Sir Henry Maine's *Village Communities in the East and West* (1871), lectures 3–5; the description of the "common fields," however, as "divided into three long strips," is, of course, inaccurate, and shows how completely the open-field system had been forgotten before it was explained afresh by Seebohm. For the Teutonic peoples Maine avowedly based his assertions on the writings of von Maurer; and von Maurer's evidence will be found stated and critically examined in Fustel de Coulanges, *Origin of Property in Land* (Engl. trans., 1891), pp. 3–62.

The theory which traces the continental equivalent of the manor back to the Roman agricultural *villa* was set forth by Fustel de Coulanges in a number of works of which none so far have been translated. A summary view of his general position is given in the short article *Fustel de Coulanges* in Palgrave's *Dictionary of Political Economy*, vol. ii.; and an independent account of agrarian conditions under the Roman empire will be found in Pelham's lecture on *The Imperial Domains and the Colonate* (1890).

Since the question was reopened by Fustel and Seebohm, much fresh light has been thrown on the whole subject of serfdom by Professor Vinogradoff (*Villainage in England*, 1892; *The Growth of the Manor*, 1905), and the late Professor Maitland (Pollock and Maitland, *History of English Law*,

Appendix

1895; *Domesday Book and Beyond*, 1897). The trend of the arguments of both is in favour of the original freedom of the main stock of cultivators of the soil; but while the former is disposed to save a good deal of the "collective ownership" involved in the "mark" doctrine, the latter is inclined to minimise every feature of an apparently "communal" character. The reader will perhaps be unable to devote much time to these books unless he wishes to make a special study of the problem of origins. But at any rate he should read the account of villein tenure in Pollock and Maitland, *History of English Law*, vol. i. bk. ii. ch. i. § 12, and the brilliant section in Maitland's *Domesday Book and Beyond*, pp. 107-128, in which it is argued that a "manor" meant originally a "house against which Danegeld was charged." Reviews of a good many recent works on agrarian history, including those of Vinogradoff and Maitland, will be found in Ashley's *Surveys, Historic and Economic* (1900). These may be useful as presenting in a brief form most of the main propositions of the works in question; but the reader will discern, and be on his guard against, any bias on the reviewer's part. The most recent attempt of the same writer to review the present position of the controversy will be found in the address on *Comparative Economic History and the English Landlord*, printed in the *Economic Journal* for June 1913.

A vast mass of information as to the details of mediæval English life was obtained by Thorold Rogers from the account rolls of bailiffs and similar documents, and is presented in his *History of Agriculture and Prices* (I. and II., 1866), and in more popular forms in his *Six Centuries of Work and Wages* (1884) and *Economic Interpretation of History* (1888). It is perhaps best studied in its first and more scholarly presentation; and chapter ii. of *Agriculture and Prices*, I., will be found a characteristic and instructive specimen of his methods, though some of the statements are open to criticism. But the relation of the particular facts to one another has only been

Economic Organisation

made clear since we have understood the real nature of the open field; and the reading of Rogers is best postponed till, by the help of Seebohm or subsequent works, the main outlines have been grasped of the agrarian organisation as a whole.

The chief contemporary sources of information on rural economy is the treatise on *Husbandry* of Walter of Henley. This, with some kindred writings, has been translated by the late Miss Lamond, with an Introduction by Dr. Cunningham (R. Hist. Soc., 1890). Pp. ix–xviii of the Introduction will be found suggestive.

The really vital part of the information as to agricultural methods derivable from Rogers and Walter of Henley is now incorporated in Prothero's *English Farming, Past and Present* (1912). For the place of open-field tillage in the evolution of agriculture out of "wild field-grass husbandry," as well as for the facts as to crops and livestock, Prothero's chapter i. should be consulted. It should be noticed that "village farm" is the writer's term for the more or less associated or joint cultivation of the manor, regarded as a whole.

There is no very good account of manorial courts. A brief statement will be found in Denton's *England in the Fifteenth Century* (1888), pp. 13–16. But the distinction there drawn between the "court baron" for freeholders and the "court customary" for villeins has been shown by Maitland and other recent writers to have been a comparatively late invention of the lawyers. Maitland's discussion of the various sources of seigneurial justice in *History of English Law*, bk. ii. ch. iii. § 5, is of fundamental importance for the serious study of the subject, but will be found difficult by those unacquainted with constitutional and legal terminology.

For the economic self-sufficiency of the manorial group, reference may be made to *Econ. Hist.*, i. pp. 33–36, and for a comparison between the modern and mediæval village to pp. 40–43.

The quotation from Lord Eversley on p. 5 is from p. 17 of

Appendix

his *Agrarian Tenures* (1893), written by him when he was Mr. Shaw Lefevre. The French and German authorities cited on p. 6 are Leonce de Lavergne, *Rural Economy of Great Britain and Ireland* (Engl. trans., 1855), p. 74, and Adolf Buchenberger, *Agrarwesen und Agrarpolitik* (1892), p. 391. For the relation between Excise and the "incidents" of feudal tenure, see Dowell, *History of Taxation* (ed. 2, 1888), ii. pp. 17–22.

LECTURE II

The most important contribution to the early history of English boroughs is the section in Maitland's *Domesday Book and Beyond*, pp. 172–219. For London reference must be made to Round, *The Commune of London* (1899), pp. 219–251. An account of recent German and French discussions as to town life on the Continent is given in Ashley, *Surveys*: see especially the article on *The Beginnings of Town Life in the Middle Ages*, and the review of von Below. Much of the recent discussion involves the use of an elaborate technical terminology; but *Surveys*, pp. 167–173, will indicate the general character of the questions involved.

The merit of having established the universality of the gild merchant in English town development belongs to the late Professor Charles Gross, and the main facts are clearly set forth in his *Gild Merchant* (1890), i. pp. 4–60. A summary view is given in *Econ. Hist.*, i. pp. 68–76, and a discussion of the relations between merchant and craft gilds in *Surveys*, pp. 213–218, 225–226.

An account of the earlier craft gilds is given in *Econ. Hist.*, i. §§ 8–11. The whole of craft history was there construed with a somewhat too exclusive attention to its earlier stages: for a fuller account of the later craft companies, and a version of their history substantially identical with that in the text, reference may be made to ii. §§ 31–36.

Economic Organisation

The most notable recent work on the subject, especially in relation to London, is Professor Unwin's *Gilds and Companies of London* (1908). Any bias of the present writer in favour of regulation and control and any tendency to emphasize the more satisfactory sides of craft organisation will be abundantly corrected by perusal of the last-named writer, who certainly gives sufficient prominence to all the monopolistic and selfish features.

As to the stages of industrial organisation: the first attempt to set forth in English the classification introduced by German scholars will be found in *Econ. Hist.*, ii. pp. 219–222. With this may now be compared Bücher, *Industrial Evolution* (1893; Engl. trans., 1901), ch. iv.; Unwin, *Industrial Organisation in the Sixteenth and Seventeenth Centuries* (1904), Intro.; and Lloyd, *The Cutlery Trades* (1913), ch. i.

The doctrine of Aquinas, the most influential of the mediæval scholastic doctors, on *Just Price*, is explained in *Econ. Hist.*, i. § 16, with which may be compared Cunningham, *Growth of English Industry and Commerce*, i. 249–255. For mediæval practice in the regulation of prices, see *Econ. Hist.*, i. §§ 20, 21; ii. § 27.

LECTURE III

The general course of Commutation is set forth in *Econ. Hist.*, i. pp. 29–33, and Vinogradoff, *Villainage*, pp. 178–183. More exact estimates than had previously been available of the extent to which commutation took place before and after the Black Death have been given by Page in his monograph on *The End of Villainage in England* (Publications of the Amer. Econ. Assoc., 1900).

The effects of compulsory labour, as witnessed by contemporary observers in central Europe about the end of the eighteenth century, are stated by Jones, *Distribution of Wealth* (1831). The chapters on *Peasant Rents*, reprinted separately

Appendix

under that title (1895), form a most suggestive commentary on mediæval English development.

For "land and stock leases" reference should be made to Thorold Rogers, *Agriculture and Prices*, i. pp. 24–25, 667–668, or *Six Centuries of Work and Wages*, pp. 277–282.

On the relation of the Black Death to the Peasant Revolt, *Econ. Hist.*, ii. 264–7, should be read in the light of Page, as above.

On the legal character of villein tenure and its relation to enclosures, the discussion was opened by *Econ. Hist.*, ii. pp. 272–283. The subject must now be viewed in the light of the discovery by Savine of instances of the intervention of the courts: see his article in *Quarterly Journal of Economics* (published by Harvard University), xix. (1904). Recent discussions of the subject, utilising Savine's new facts, will be found in Johnson, *The Disappearance of the Small Landowner* (1909), pp. 62–72, and Tawney, *The Agrarian Problem in the Sixteenth Century* (1912), pp. 287–301, and the reviews by the present writer of the former work in *Econ. Journal* (1910), xx. p. 54, and of the later, *ibid.* (1913), xxiii. p. 85.

A first rough attempt was made to estimate the geographical extent of the Tudor enclosures in *Econ. Hist.*, ii. pp. 286–288 (see the notes and map). This must now be considerably modified in the light of Gay, *Inclosures in England in the Sixteenth Century*, in *Quarterly Journal of Economics* (1903), xvii. Gay's percentages have been presented in the form of a map by Mr. Johnson in his book above mentioned; but see the criticism already referred to.

A synopsis of the Tudor legislation concerning enclosures is given in Appendix D to Slater's *The English Peasantry and the Enclosure of the Common Fields* (1907); and there is a valuable account of government intervention and a discussion of its effects in Tawney's book before mentioned, pp. 351–400.

The quotation from Hallam on p. 66 is from his *Constitutional History* (8vo ed.), 1, p. 79.

Economic Organisation

LECTURE IV

The characteristics of the period of "town economy" are explained by Schmoller, with special reference to German development, in *The Mercantile System* (Engl. trans., 1896), pp. 1–13; and the subject is dealt with at some length in relation to England in *Econ. Hist.*, i. § 13; ii. §§ 24–29.

An account of the Hanseatic Steelyard in London is given in Pauli's *Pictures of Old England* (Engl. trans.).

Fresh light has been thrown on the early history of the London Great Companies, and on the position of the foreign commercial element in the thirteenth century, by Unwin, *Gilds and Companies of London*, chapters iv. to vi. For the fourteenth and fifteenth centuries a more vivid impression is to be obtained from turning over the London documents translated by Riley in *Memorials of London and London Life* (1868) than from any modern writings.

The relation of Risk to the mediæval doctrine of Usury is briefly stated in *Econ. Hist.*, ii. p. 419, and the subject discussed more at length in Cunningham, *English Industry and Commerce*, i. pp. 360–368; while the history of the conception of Capital in business practice and in economic theory will be found in the article under that head by the present writer in *An Encyclopædia of Industrialism* (1913).

Dr. Scott's *Joint Stock Companies to 1720* (1911–12) contains a most valuable collection of material for the commercial history of the sixteenth and seventeenth centuries, which economists have only just begun to utilise. For the lines of development converging on the first English joint stock companies, chapter i. should be read; and for the peculiar significance of the Russia Company, chapter ii. With this may be compared the similar experience later of the East India Company, as narrated in Hunter's *History of British India* (1899), i., chapters vi. and vii.

Appendix

LECTURE V

The early development of the English woollen industry is given at some length in *Econ. Hist.*, ii. ch. iii.; which may now be supplemented on the technical side by Salzmann, *English Industries of the Middle Ages* (1913), pp. 141–156. The part played by *Alien Immigrants* is the subject of a special work under that title by Dr. Cunningham (1897): for the Flemish weavers of the fourteenth century see § 22, and for the Walloons and Flemings of the sixteenth century §§ 29–35.

The intention and effects of the Justices' Assessments were first dealt with, in recent times, by Thorold Rogers; see for instance his *Economic Interpretation of History*, pp. 38–45. The problem was more dispassionately considered, and fresh evidence adduced, by Hewins, *English Trade and Finance, chiefly in the Seventeenth Century* (1892), pp. 82–88, and Cunningham, *English Industry and Commerce* (1903), ii. § 168. It is to be hoped that the two most instructive papers on the subject by Mr. Tawney, in English though published in the *Vierteljahrschrift für Social- und Wirtschaftsgeschichte* (1913), will soon be accessible in an English publication.

The early history of the Poor Law is given in *Econ. Hist.*, ii. ch. v.; and its development under Elizabeth and the first two Stuarts by Miss Leonard, *The Early History of English Poor Relief* (1900). The latter book is indispensable for a just view of Tudor and Stuart conceptions of statecraft, and for the part played by the Council.

List's view of "productive powers," referred to on p. 90, is set forth by him in his *National System of Political Economy* (Engl. trans., new ed., 1904), ch. xii. The pamphleteer referred to on p. 94 was Dr. Arbuthnot, whose *History of John Bull* is conveniently accessible in Cassell's National Library.

Economic Organisation

LECTURE VI

The best introduction to the agrarian history of the eighteenth century is still Toynbee's *Industrial Revolution of the Eighteenth Century* (1884), cheap ed., pp. 13–22, 34–44, though it can now be supplemented and corrected in detail by reference to more recent works, such as Johnson's *Disappearance of the Small Landowner*, especially pp. 128-150. The movements for improvement in agricultural methods are described fully in Prothero's *English Farming, Past and Present*, chapters vii.–xi. Two recent and extremely instructive treatises on the mechanism and consequences of enclosure are those of J. L. and B. Hammond, *The Village Labourer* (1911), and Professor Gonner, *Common Land and Inclosure*. Their attitude is very different, and they produce different impressions. A useful criticism and comparison of the two by J. H. Clapham will be found in the *Economic Journal*, June 1912, with which may be compared Slater, *Making of Modern England* (1913), pp. 37–43. For the effect of the Corn Laws the reader will do well to turn to Nicholson's *History of the English Corn Laws* (1904). The views of agricultural experts and of economists with regard to the superiority of large over small farming, and a discussion of the bearing of their arguments on cereal farming in particular, occupy Part I of Professor Levy's *Large and Small Holdings* (Engl. trans., 1911). An approximation to really significant statistics as to the size of holdings was made for the first time in 1914: see *Agricultural Statistics*, xlviii, pt. 1.

The most readable and compact account of the history of English land law, up to the devising of the present method of Family Settlement, is in Sir Frederick Pollock's *Land Laws*, chapters iii.–v.

The Whig authority quoted on p. 127 is Brodrick, *English Land and English Landlords* (1881), p. 99; and the well-

Appendix

known writer of the west country of p. 131 is Mr. Baring-Gould, *Old Country Life* (1889), cheap ed., 1913, p. 15.

LECTURE VII

It would be a mistake to begin the study of the Industrial Revolution elsewhere than in the pages of Toynbee's book of that name, chapters ii., iv., vi., viii.; and for the changes in mechanical methods Jevons' *Coal Question* (1865), chapter vi., should not be neglected. But after the general view obtained from these books it will be well to go on to the more thorough discussion of many of the questions involved in Archdeacon Cunningham's *Growth of English Industry and Commerce* (1903), iii. §§ 242-272.

The effect upon the formation of capital of the religious ideas of the Calvinists was first pointed out by Max Weber, and the argument was further elaborated by Ernst Troeltsch. None of their writings are so far accessible in English. The same line of thought, however, has been applied to England by Professor Levy in his *Economic Liberalism*, ch. v. (Engl. trans., 1913); and a few pages by the present writer on the subject appear in the *British Association Handbook to Birmingham* (1913), pp. 354-358.

Of capitalism in manufactures in the seventeenth century some examples are given by Levy, *Monopoly and Competition* (Engl. trans., 1911), ch. i. Karl Marx's analysis of what he calls "manufacture" will be found in *Capital*, ch. xxiv.

A brief account of industrial legislation in the nineteenth century is given in Jevons' *State in Relation to Labour* (1882); and a fuller statement in Hutchins and Harrison, *History of Factory Legislation* (2nd ed., 1911): while the best account of the early history of labour combinations will be found in the earlier chapters (more objective, perhaps, in their tone than the later) of Mr. and Mrs. Webb's *History of Trade*

Economic Organisation

Unionism (1894). An impartial abstract of the Report of the Poor Law Commission of 1832, indicating the evils in the working of the system of relief adopted at the end of the previous century, will be found in the Report of the recent Poor Law Commission (1909), pt. iii.

The chapter (vii.) devoted to the problem of what he calls "trade union structure" in Mr. Cole's *World of Labour* (1913) is one of the most instructive parts of a work which makes up by its vivacity and width of reading for its onesidedness and occasional violence of language.

The Halifax letters referred to on p. 148 are printed in *The Letter Books of Joseph Holroyd and Sam Hill*, ed. Heaton (Halifax, 1914).

LECTURE VIII

After reading Mill's enthusiastic and hopeful account of productive co-operation in his *Political Economy*, bk. iv. ch. vii. § 6, it is desirable to study the subsequent history of the experiments in this direction in Potter (Mrs. Webb), *The Co-operative Movement in Great Britain* (1891), ch. v., and Schloss, *Methods of Industrial Remuneration* (ed. 3, 1898), chapters xxii.-xxiv. An account and estimate of "distributive co-operation," with its large number of retail stores, its Co-operative Wholesale Society and the factories which the latter owns, is given in Price, *Co-operation and Co-partnership*, chapters viii.-x. On productive co-operation, in the later form which it has taken at Kettering and elsewhere, there is a paper, *Co-operation in England* (1899), by the present writer, reprinted in *Surveys*, pp. 399-404.

The recent experiments in the direction of Co-partnership —meaning thereby a plan by which the whole or part of the worker's share of profit is invested in the concern employing him—are sympathetically described by Fay, *Copartnership in*

Appendix

Industry (1913), ch. iii., and analysed in Mr. Price's work above mentioned, pp. 220-259. The whole subject of Profit-sharing and Co-partnership is considered in an article, *Profit-sharing*, by the present writer in the *Quarterly Review* for October 1913.

The views of Auguste Comte on the labour question may be conveniently studied in his *General View of Positivism* (1848), ch. iii., Engl. trans. by Bridges, p. 117.

A quite indispensable collection of facts with regard to the modern tendency towards capitalistic combination and monopoly is Macrosty's *Trust Movement in British Industry* (1907); where chapter ii. on the iron and steel industries and chapter v. on the textile industries bear closely on the argument of this lecture. The history of railway amalgamations and the extent of combination between the great lines are briefly treated in Ross, *British Railways* (1904), chapters i. and ii. The organisation of the *Shipping Conferences* is explained, and the problem considered "in what sense and to what extent a Shipping Conference making use of the system of deferred rebates secures a monopoly" in the *Report of the Royal Commission on Shipping Rings* (1909). "Existing monopolist organisations in English industry" are described in Levy, *Monopoly and Competition* (Engl. trans., 1911), ch. ix., and the reasons for their growth considered in ch. x.

The facts as to the wide diffusion of the ownership of many great modern undertakings, and the argument based upon them, formed perhaps the most striking part of the famous book by Eduard Bernstein, *Die Voraussetzungen des Sozialismus* (1899), which precipitated the controversy between the Revisionist and the Marxian schools of German socialists. They will be found at pp. 40-54 of the Eng. trans. (1909) under the title *Evolutionary Socialism*.

Professor Otto Gierke's teaching as to the nature of "Genossenschaften" (Communities and Corporations) was introduced to English readers by Professor Maitland's trans-

Economic Organisation

lation of a portion of his great work, under the title of *Political Theories of the Middle Ages* (1900), preceded by a preface in which Maitland showed, in passing, its bearing on modern discussions as to the nature of labour organisations. Since then the general conception has had a growing influence, and it has begun to affect political speculation, as may be seen in Mr. Lindsay's article on *The State in Recent Political Theory* in the *Political Quarterly* for February 1914.

INDEX

Italics indicate more or less technical terms, as well as the titles of books.

Abstinence, 157
Accidents, insurance against, 168
Acre, shape and size of, 15
Addison, 122
Adults, restriction of labour of, 164 *seq.*
Adventurers, Merchant, 76, 84, 85, 115, 116
Advertisement, 185
Alva, 90
Amalgamation of business, 185
Amsterdam, 148
Ancient Law, 167
Antwerp, 77, 78
Apprentice, 38
Apprenticeship, 38, 42, 100, 164
Apprentices, statute of, 92, 96, 100, 102 *seq.*, 164
Appurtenant, 11
Aquinas, 198
Arbuthnot, Dr., 201
Aristotle, 19
Armstrong & Co., 184
Assessment of wages, 102 *seq.*, 107, 164
Associations, 186
Atlantic steamships, 185
Austria, 48

BACON, Lord Chancellor, 62, 113, 114
Bailiff, 12, 46, 54
Bakewell, 135
Balk, 14
Bank of England, 125
Banks, country, 156
Baring-Gould, S., 202
Barley, 14
Baxter, Richard, 158
Bavaria, 121
Beans, 14
Bedfordshire, 63
Belfast, 190

Belgium, 185
Bentham, Jeremy, 137
Bergen, 72
Bernstein, E., 205
Biology, 168
Black Death, 49 *seq.*, 97
Blackwell Hall, 91, 94, 116
Blast-furnaces, 182, 184
Bleachers, 186, 187
Board of Trade, 108, 164
Boards, Trade, 107, 169
Book of Common Prayer, 97, 99
Boonday, 12, 49
Boot manufacture, 145
Bourse, Berlin, 128
Boynton, 151
Bradford, 146, 148, 186, 187
Breeches, manufacture of, 145
Breweries, 182
Brian, C. J., 61
Bridgman, Orlando, 127
Briggs, Messrs., 176
Bright, John, 166, 170
Brodrick, G., 202
Brotherhood, 30
Brown & Co., 184
Bruges, 72, 77
Bucks, 63
Burleigh, Lord, 169
Burns, Robert, 17

CALAIS, 75, 76
Calico Printers' Association, 186
Calling, 158
Calvinism, 158
Canals, 155
Canonist lawyers, 82
Capital, 79, 82, 141, 148, 155 *seq.*, 174, 176, 180 *seq.*; capitals, 157; fixed, 181; ownership of, 182
Capitalism, 173, 181 *seq.*

207

Economic Organisation

Carlyle, Thomas, 160
Carnegie, 183
Cash-nexus, 160
Catechism, 99
Chantry, 30
Charles I., 112, 114, 116
Chartism, 160
Chaucer, 54
Child, Sir Josiah, 162
Children, hours of labour of, 164
China, 34, 69, 71
Church, teaching on Usury, 82
Clapham, J. H., 202
Climate, 11
Cloth, woollen, 76, 87, 146, 162
Clothiers, 92 *seq.*, 115 *seq.*, 143, 148, 150
Clove, 71
Clover, 135
Clydebank Shipbuilding Company, 184
Coal-mining, 154, 155, 165
Coal Question, 140
Coke, Sir Edward, 61, 97
Coke of Holkham, 135
Colbert, 152, 163
Cole, G. D. H., 204
Collective action, of capital, 181, 189 *seq.*
Collective bargaining, 169 *seq.*
Cologne, 71
Combination, of labour, 160; laws, 170; of capital, 181, 184 *seq.*
Commenda, 83
Commissions, Royal, 60, 114, 170
Commission-system, 143
Common Recovery, 126
Common, rights of, 22
Commons, enclosure of, 138
Communal elements, 21, 195
Commutation, 46 *seq.*, 52
Compensation Act, Workmen's, 168
Competition, 64, 185, 187
Comte, Auguste, 178, 205
Concentration, 181 *seq.*
Conferences, Railway and Shipping, 187
Convocation, 122
Co-operation, 174 *seq.*
Co-operative Wholesale Society, 176
Copyhold, 61 *seq.*, 67, 131 *seq.*
Corn laws, 136, 166
Cornwall, 151
Corporate organisation of industry, 190
Correction, house of, 109

Cost of living, 105, 109
Cottar, 17
Cotton industry, 100, 145, 153, 160, 182
Council, Privy, 96, 103, 111 *seq.*, 114 *seq.*, 120, 164
Counter-Reformation, 121
County Councils, 129
Court, manorial, 23, 51, 110
Coventry, 107
Craft, 28; modern application of term, 172
Crises, 115, 189
Cromwell, Oliver, 66
Crown lands, 121
Cunningham, Archdeacon, 193, 196, 200, 201, 203
Currants, 85
Custom, 45
Customary tenants, 44

DANGEROUS trades, 165
Darwinism, 168
Debasement of currency, 66
De Donis, statute, 126
Defoe, Daniel, 144
Demesne, 12, 16; letting of, 53 *seq.*
Derwent, 153
Devonshire, 92, 130, 151
Discourse of Trade, 162
Disraeli, 66
Dissenters, 158
Docks, London, 190
Domesday Survey, 9
Domestic system, 36, 93, 142 *seq.*, 155, 181
Drapers, 81, 91, 93
Dream of John Ball, 49
Durham, 190
Dutch, 162
Duty of a Steward to his Lord, 124
Dyers, 89, 186

EAST India Company, 84, 124
Economies, internal, 180; of combination, 185
Economists, 79, 138, 156, 170
Edinburgh Review, 138
Education Office, 164
Edward III, 95
Edward VI, 66, 102, 115
Elizabeth, Queen, 133, 164, 169
Embezzlement of material, 145
Enclosure, 56 *seq.*, 114, 137 *seq.*
Engineering, strike of 1897, 171; Federation, 189
English Sewing Cotton Company, 182

Index

Entail, 125
Essex, 92, 105
Eversley, Lord, 5, 122, 196
Excise, 11

FACTORIES (=trading settlements), 72
Factory system, 36, 93, 149, 154, 159 *seq.*, 173; factory acts, 164 *seq.*, 179, 181
Factors, 148
Factor-system, 143, 155
Family system, 36
Farmer, original sense of term, 54, 64
Farms, large and small, 138; amalgamation of, 139
Fay, C. R, 204
Federation of Engineering and Shipbuilding Employers, 189
Feldzwang, 14
Felt industry, 145
Fencing of machinery, 165
Ferm, 54
Fideicommisse, 127
Field, 13
Fine, on admission to customary tenements, 59; on renewal of leases, 133
Fine Cotton Spinners, 182, 186
Fitzherbert, 132
Fixed capital, 181
Flanders galleys, 73
Flax, manufactures of, 145
Flat, 15
Fondaco dei Tedeschi, 72
Foreigner, 70
Four-course rotation, 135
France, peasant proprietors in, 3; apprenticeship in, 38; silk industry of, 94; 112, 114, 139, 185
Fraternity, 29, 30, 33
Frederick the Great, 120
Freedom of Contract, 161
Free-holder, 17
Frohnden, 48
From Status to Contract, 167
Fullers, 89
Furlong, two senses, 15
Fur manufacture, 145
Fustel de Coulanges, 194
Fustian manufacture, 145

GAUL, 20
Gay, E. F., 199
Geldwirthschaft, 45
Germany, peasant proprietors in, 2; labour dues in, 48; 69, 95, 112, 185

Ghent, 90, 112
Gierke, Professor Otto, 191, 205
Gild, mediæval sense of, 29
Gild merchant, 27
Gild system, 25, 28 *seq.*, 36, 39 *seq.* 181
Gilpin, Bernard, 60
Glasgow, 190
Glass manufacture, 151
Gloucester, 106
Glove manufacture, 145
Gneist, Professor, 128
Goldsmiths, 80
Gonner, Professor, 202
Grande Industrie, 144
Green, J. R., 101
Green, T. H., 167
Gross, Professor Charles, 197
Groups, social, 191
Guest, Keen & Nettlefold, 184

HALIFAX, 146, 148
Hallam, Henry, 66
Halls, cloth, 146
Halsbury, Lord Chancellor, 188
Hamburg, 86, 148
Hammond, J. L. and B., 202
Handicraft system, 36
Handloom, 149, 155, 160
Hanse, Teutonic, 71 *seq.*, 86, 92
Hat manufacture, 145
Hay, 22
Hedges, 56
Hegel, 167
Hemp, manufactures of, 145
Henry II, 95
Henry VII, 83, 113
Henry VIII, 66, 96, 102, 121
Herring fishery, 71
Hewins, W. A. S., 201
Holbein, 86
Holland, 94
Home Office, 164
Hosiery industry, 149
House industry, 36, 93
Household system, 36
Huddersfield, 146, 147
Huguenots, 125
Husbandland, 14
Huxley, 168

INCIDENTS of tenure in chivalry, 10
Individualism, 64, 167, 168, 191
Industries, 172
Inspectorate, 164
Instrument of production, 146

Economic Organisation

Insurance Act, 169
Integration, 181, 183 seq.
Intermixed holdings, 21
International agreements in business, 185
Invention, conditions of, 155
Investment, 79, 141
Ireland, 167
Iron industry, 100, 145
Italy, 69, 95, 114

JEVONS, W. S., 140, 155, 168, 203
John Bull, 94, 201
Johnson, A. H., 199, 202
Joint-stock, 83, 84, 117, 179 seq.
Jones, Richard, 198
Journeymen, 38, 41
Justices of the Peace, 97 seq.; assessments of wages, 101 seq.; and poor relief, 111
Just price, 41, 198

KING, Gregory, 119, 123
Knapp, Professor, 120
Krupp, 183

LABOUR Co-partnership, 176
Labour dues, mediæval, 12
Labour question, 42
Labourers, characteristics of English agricultural, 4, 5, 17; statute of, 50; justices of, 97
Laissez Faire, 167, 168
Land Tax Assessments, 124
Landed interest, 125
Landlords, number of English, 3; characteristics of, 3; 134
Langland, William, 101
Latimer, 65
Laud, Archbishop, 114
Laurence, Edward, 124, 133, 134
Law and order, 161
Leases, 53 seq., 58, 67, 132 seq.
Leather industry, 145
Leeds, 146, 147
Leicestershire, 63, 91
Leonard, Miss, 201
Levant Company, 86
Levy, Professor, 202, 203, 205
Limited liability, 179
Limited partnership, 83
Lincolnshire, 91
Lindsay, A. D., 206
Linen manufacture, 94, 145
Lipton's, 182
List, Frederick, 90, 201

Livesey, Sir George, 177
Living, 14
Local Government Board, 164
Locke, John, 161, 163, 167
London, 32, 38, 72, 80, 107, 174, 190
Louis XIV, 163
Low Countries, 56, 73, 111
Lübeck, 71
Luther, 112

MACAULAY, 125
Macclesfield, 107
M'Culloch, 138
Machinery, 154 seq., 160 seq.
Macrosty, H. W., 205
Maine, Sir Henry, 167, 194
Maitland, F. W., 49, 195, 196, 197, 205
Make, 182
Malmesbury Abbey, 150
Malmsey wine, 85
Manchester, 170, 187
Man v. the State, 191
Manor, 8 seq., 110
Mantoux, M., 140
Manufacture, 149
Manufactures, royales and *privilegiées*, 152
Manure, 22
Mark theory, 20, 195
Markets, 46; market in economic sense, 36
Marx, Karl, 149, 152, 183
Master, 38, 93
Maurer, Georg von, 194
Mercers, 81
Merchant Gild, 27
Merchant Shipping Act, 165
Métayer, 4, 55
Middle class, 26, 183
Middlesex, 63
Mill, John Stuart, 7, 157, 168, 174
Miners, minimum wage of, 108
Minimum Wage Act, 169
Mistery, 28
Mogul case, 188
Mohair manufacture, 145
Monasteries, dissolution of, 66, 121
Money economy, 45
Moneyed interest, 125
Monopolies, 152, 184, 188, 189; monopoly prices, 189
Monuments in churches, 131
Moralisation of employers, 179 seq.
More, Sir Thomas, 59, 113, 114
Morgen, 15

Index

Morris, William, 49
Morton, Archbishop, 83

NAPOLEONIC wars, 87, 136
Natural economy, 45
Naturalwirthschaft, 45
Newcastle, 184
Nicholson, Professor, 202
Nonconformists, 158
Non-textile factories, 166
Norfolk, 92; rotation, 135
Northamptonshire, 63
Norwich, 148
Novgorod, 72
Nucleated village, 12

OATS, 14
Occupations, 172
Open field, 13
Osney Abbey, 150
Overseers of the poor, 111, 118
Oxen, in ploughing, 15, 23; weight of, 135
Oxfordshire, 63, 124

PAGE, T. W., 198
Pageants, 30
Paris, 174
Parish, as unit of administration, 110
Parliament, under Tudors, 96
Parliamentary Government, 7, 120 *seq.*, 129 *seq.*
Parsimony, 157
Partnership, 83 *seq.*
Passive trade, 69
Pasture farming, 56 *seq.*
Patronage, 130
Pauli, Reinhold, 129, 200
Peace, Justices of, 97 *seq.*, 128, 129
Peas, 14
Peasant protection, 120
Peasants' Revolt, 49 *seq.*
Pepperers, 81
Philosophy, social, 161, 167, 191
Piers the Plowman, 101
Pins, manufacture of, 149, 153
Plague, Great, 49 *seq.*
Plant, cost of, 186
Plimsoll line, 166
Political Economy, 138, 167, 170
Pollock, Sir Frederick, 202
Poor Law, 96, 110 *seq.*, 117, 136, 159
Population in 1688 and 1769, 119; in 1801 and 1901, 173
Postlethwayt, Malachy, 145
Power, 153

Price, L. L., 204
Prices, rise of, 66; control of, 184; monopoly, 189
Primogeniture, 127
Productive powers, 90
Profit-sharing, 176
Prothero, R. E., 196, 202
Property, doctrine of, 163
Protection, 186
Prussia, 127

QUARTER Sessions, 97, 102, 129

RADICALS, 139, 170
Railways, 155; Conferences, 187
Railway servants, hours of, 165
Reeve, 12, 54
Reformation, 7, 64
Reform Bill of 1832, 141
Report of 1806, 142, 146, 150; of 1894, 170
Revolution of 1688, 119, 120, 161, 163
Revolution, the industrial, 140 *seq.*, 156
Ricardo, David, 156
Rittergut, 19
Rogers, Thorold, 49 *seq.*, 55 *seq.*, 195, 199, 201
Roman agrarian system, 20
Rotation of crops, 14, 22
Rotterdam, 148
Russia, 69, 185
Russia Company, 84
Rutlandshire, 63
Rye, 14

SAVINE, A., 199
Schmoller, Professor, 200
Scott, Sir Walter, 40
Scott, W. R., 200
Screws, 184
Seamen, contracts of, 165
Seebohm, Frederic, 193
Seigneurial elements, 23
Seigneurie, 19
Self-Government, 129
Sempstresses, 146
Senior, N. W., 157
Serfdom, 18, 19
Settlement, Parish, 109
Settlements, Family or Strict, 125 *seq.*
Sewing-machine, 146, 149
Shaftesbury, Lord, 166
Shakespeare, 99

211

Economic Organisation

Shares, transference of, 179
Sheep-breeding, 56 seq., 135
Sheffield, 184
Shipbuilding, 184; Federation, 189
Shipping Conferences, 187
Shoe manufacture, 145
Shot, 15
Sickness, insurance against, 169
Silesia, 94, 128
Silk manufacture, 94, 125, 145; spinning, 153
Silver, influx of, 102
Slater, G., 199
Slavery, 18
Smith, Adam, 35, 141, 149, 156, 157, 163
Smithfield market, 135
Soap manufacture, 151
Socialism, 191
Societas, 83
Socmen, 17
Solidarity, sense of, 189 seq.
Somerset, 92
Sorbonne, 112
Sound, the, 72
Southampton, 73
South Metropolitan Gas Company, 177
Spectator, 122
Spencer, Herbert, 168
Spices, 68
Spiritual power, 178
Spitalfields Acts, 107
Squire, the, 5 seq., 122, 131
Staffordshire, 184
Stages of industrial evolution, 34 seq.
Staple, Merchants of the, 74 seq.
State control, 161 seq.
Statutes :—
    1285 (De Donis), 126
    1351 (Labourers), 50
    1465 (Clothiers), 92
    1489 (Husbandry), 114
    1536 (Poor Relief), 110
    1555 (,, ,,), 111
    1555 (Weavers), 150
    1563 (Poor Relief), 111
    1563 (Wages, Apprenticeship), 92, 96, 100, 102 seq., 107, 164
    1572 (Poor Relief), 111
    1585 (Cloth), 151
    1597-8 (Wages), 103
    1598 (Vagrancy), 109
    1601 (Poor Relief), 96
    1603-4 (Wages), 104

Statutes (*continued*)—
    1702 ⎫
    1710 ⎬ (Embezzlement), 145
    1740 ⎪
    1749 ⎭
    1756 ⎱ (Weavers), 106
    1757 ⎰
    1773 (Spitalfields), 107
    1813 (Wages), 164
    1814 (Apprenticeship), 164
    1819 (Factories), 164
    1824 ⎱ (Combination), 170
    1825 ⎰
    1833 (Factories), 164
    1842 (Mines), 164
    1844 (Factories), 164
    1847 (Ten Hours), 166
    1875 (Shipping), 165
    1893 (Railways), 165
    1897 (Workmen's Compensation), 168
    1908 (Eight Hours), 165
    1909 (Trade Boards), 107, 169
    1911 (Insurance), 169
    1912 (Minimum Wage) 108, 169
Steam-engine, 155
Steamship companies, 185
Steel, manufacture of, 183; rails, 185, 187
Steelyard, 72, 86
Stock, leased with land, 55
Stock, joint, 83, 84, 179 seq.
Strickland, Sir George, 151
Struggle for existence, 168
Suffolk, 92
Supply and Demand, 101
Surveying, 132
Survival of the fittest, 168
Sweated trades, 107
Swift, Jonathan, 125
Sybil, 66
Syndicalism, 191

TAILORING industry, 181
Tailors, Merchant, 80
Taltarum's case, 126
Tar, 68
Tawney, R. H., 199, 201
Team, eight-ox, 23
Tenant, 9
Tenant farmers, characteristics of English, 4; origin of, 53 seq., 64
Tenant-right, 134
Ten Hours Act, 166
Tenters, 162
Territorial law, 70

Index

Textile trades, 164, 165, 186
Thorough, 112, 114
Tiverton, 150
Tobacco business, 185
Tool and *Machine*, 149
Tories, 139, 166
Tours, 119, 137, 151
Town (=village), 11
Towns, early history of, 26
Town-economy, 95
Townshend, Lord, 135
Toynbee, Arnold, 128, 140, 203
Trade, Board of, 108, 164
Trade Boards, 107, 169
Trade Unions, 170 *seq.*, 177
Transportation, 155
Troilus and Cressida, 99
Trusts, 186 *seq.*
Tucker, 92
Tudor period, characteristics of, 89 *seq.*
Turnips, 135
Turnpike roads, 155

ULSTER, 134
Umpire, 171
Undertaker, 149
Unemployment, 115, 118, 169
Unions, trade, 170 *seq.*
United States, 185
Universal Dictionary of Trade and Commerce, 145
Unwin, Professor, 198, 200
Usury, 82
Utopia, 59

VAGRANCY, 109
Values in exchange, 90
Venice, 71, 73, 85
Verlagsystem, 142
Verleger, 142
View of craft, 31
Villa theory, 20
Villein, meaning of, 13
Villeinage, land in, 12
Vinogradoff, Professor, 194, 198
Virgate, 14
Visitations, heraldic, 130

WAGES, assessment of, 102 *seq.*, 107, 164; Boards, 171
Wakefield, 146
Wales, 23; South, 184
Walker, 92
Walter of Henley, 196
Warwickshire, 63
Watt, James, 37, 141
Wealth of Nations, 141
Weavers, immigration of foreign, 56, 90; gilds of, 89; legislation concerning, 106, 150
Weavers' Act (1555), 150
Webb, S. and B., 203
Week work, 13
Welfare programmes, 180
Wesley, John, 159
West Country, 12, 130
West Riding, 144, 146
Wheat, 14; price of, 137
Whig government, 129 *seq.*, 162; doctrine, 161
Whittington, 81
Wiltshire, 92
Winchcombe, John, 150
Wine, 68
Wire manufacture, 151
Wolsey, Cardinal, 116, 117
Women, restriction of labour of, 164
Wool, 56, 68, 137; export of, 88
Woollen industry, 56, 88 *seq.*, 115, 125, 145, 150, 153, 160; report of 1806 on, 142, 146
Workmen's Compensation Act, 168
Works, iron and engineering, 154, 173, 181
Wyclif, 51

Yardland, 14
Yardling, 18
Yarn, 155
Yeoman, 122
Yorkshire, 142 *seq.*, 147, 151
Young, Arthur, 119, 123, 137
Young Persons, hours of labour of, 164
Ypres, 90, 112

ZWINGLI, 112

www.ingramcontent.com/pod-product-compliance
Lightning Source LLC
LaVergne TN
LVHW041615070426
835507LV00008B/255